THE ACTOR'S CAREER BIBLE

THE ACTOR'S CAREER BIBLE

Auditioning, Networking, Survival and Success

ROB OSTLERE

methuen | drama

LONDON • NEW YORK • OXFORD • NEW DELHI • SYDNEY

METHUEN DRAMA
Bloomsbury Publishing Plc
50 Bedford Square, London, WC1B 3DP, UK
1385 Broadway, New York, NY 10018, USA

BLOOMSBURY, METHUEN DRAMA and the Methuen Drama logo are
trademarks of Bloomsbury Publishing Plc

First published in Great Britain 2019
Reprinted 2019, 2020

Copyright © Rob Ostlere, 2019

Rob Ostlere has asserted his right under the Copyright, Designs and Patents Act,
1988, to be identified as author of this work.

For legal purposes the Acknowledgements on p. vii constitute an extension of
this copyright page.

Cover images © Shutterstock

All rights reserved. No part of this publication may be reproduced or
transmitted in any form or by any means, electronic or mechanical,
including photocopying, recording, or any information storage or retrieval
system, without prior permission in writing from the publishers.

Bloomsbury Publishing Plc does not have any control over, or responsibility for,
any third-party websites referred to or in this book. All internet addresses given
in this book were correct at the time of going to press. The author and publisher
regret any inconvenience caused if addresses have changed or sites have ceased
to exist, but can accept no responsibility for any such changes.

A catalogue record for this book is available from the British Library.

A catalog record for this book is available from the Library of Congress.

ISBN: PB: 978-1-4725-8531-8
ePDF: 978-1-4725-8533-2
eBook: 978-1-4725-8532-5

Typeset by Newgen KnowledgeWorks Pvt. Ltd., Chennai, India
Printed and bound in Great Britain

To find out more about our authors and books visit www.bloomsbury.com
and sign up for our newsletters.

CONTENTS

PART ONE THE BASICS

PART TWO FINDING WORK

ACKNOWLEDGEMENTS

Thank you to all the interviewees and contributors to this guide, who gave their time and shared their insights; to Lloyd Trott for supporting the book throughout the entire process and staff at RADA for their help with many aspects of putting the book together; to Lizzie Aaryn-Stanton for editing advice and to the many others who provided feedback; to the team at Bloomsbury, for supporting the idea and the process; to Will Peterson; and to family and friends for their advice, support and patience.

INTRODUCTION

If you could ask a top casting director one question about how to get an acting job, what would it be? How about if you could quiz an industry-leading agent on the best way to get on their books? Or an experienced photographer about how to get the perfect headshot?

Now, what if you had the chance to speak to a group of more than 75 casting directors, agents, producers, directors, industry experts and a range of experienced and successful actors – what would you want to know about surviving and succeeding in the profession?

This unique guide asks (and answers!) all those questions for you. Unlike other books and blogs that focus on one person's advice, *The Actor's Career Bible* offers unprecedented access to the industry, bringing together a huge range of insiders and sharing their guidance on the attitudes, habits and know-how you need to build a successful career.

++++++

When I left RADA in 2008, I found myself on the same shaky ground as many of my friends and other actors I was meeting. We'd been thrust into an industry we didn't fully understand and were all left with the same questions: How do you get the attention of casting directors and agents? How do you deal with the pressure of auditions? What actually is networking? How do you sort out tax, find a second job, and stay upbeat when things get hard?

Without any help to guide us we flip-flopped between being passive – praying for the phone to ring – and being 'proactive!' – which sounded great but usually meant spending lots of time, money and energy without a plan and ending up with very few results. Sometimes we were lucky, sometimes we weren't, but there was never really a clear reason why, and there didn't seem to be any other option but to carry on struggling and try to stay afloat in the meantime.

Having picked up this guide, this may all sound familiar to you. Perhaps the only thing that has changed for young performers since is the growing number of acting-related blogs, podcasts, Twitter feeds, career advisors and industry conventions. This hasn't necessarily made things easier though. First of all, the mind-boggling range of expert opinions out there can easily leave you feeling muddled. Second, much of the advice centres around phrases such as, 'you are your own brand and business'. Like many actors, you may well be sick of hearing that; after all, you didn't get into performing to become a business person (and if you're honest, probably aren't really sure what the word 'brand' actually means). The third major problem with acting advice is that it often creates an unattainable ideal: the 'super-actor' who spends their day rifling off emails, building a website, running a social media marketing campaign, networking all over the place ... and then stays up all night learning lines for their audition the next morning. This is not easy to live up to if you have to work a week of bar-shifts and wouldn't mind seeing your family and friends once in a while. All of this is not to say there isn't good advice out there. But it's clear that for a long time actors have needed something else: ideas that can be tailored to their individual situation and personality, based on the realities of starting a career as a performer, collected together in one place.

So, a few years after graduating I made it my aim to speak to people in the industry directly, collect as many opinions as possible and use their advice to organize those opinions in a way that was simple to follow. The goal was to lay out everything a drama student needed to do before entering the industry; to show people coming into the profession via other routes all the ways they can get a foothold and begin to find work; to guide actors through everything they could do in the early years of their career to create the best foundations going forward; and to provide inspiration and advice for more experienced actors who were stuck in a rut ... effectively, the book that myself and other young performers were crying out for ten years ago.

I began by interviewing recent RADA graduates, and then actors from other drama schools and universities and professional actors who hadn't trained. As well as lots of tips, I found out the common problems people face early in their careers; from big topics like how to find the right headshot photographer, down to small details like what subject heading to use in an email to an agent. Then, with the help of senior staff at RADA, I interviewed people from across the industry, including agents, casting directors, producers, directors, photographers, showreel editors, career advisors, accountants and staff at Equity and Spotlight – all the people involved in an actor's career. I spoke to professionals at the top of British TV, film and theatre, as well as people with experience at every other level of the industry, with the aim of leaving no stone unturned. Crucially, all these interviews were conducted confidentially, with each person comfortable enough to speak their mind and not sugar-coat any of the harsher realities of the profession.

Everything you read in *The Actor's Career Bible* comes from those interviews, offering solutions you can tailor to your situation and career stage, without requiring you to be business minded or have loads of spare hours or cash. Work on the essentials and follow the insider tips on how to get ahead, and using this guide you can build the foundations for a successful career and life as an actor.

For free resources to help you make the most of the expert advice in this chapter, visit www.actorscareerbible.com/freestuff

USING THIS GUIDE

A guide to terms used in the book

While all quotes are anonymous, basic details are included about the profession of the person giving advice and also, where relevant, the level of the industry they're working at and/or which medium they specialize in.

Actor/s: used for performers of all genders.

Casting teams: a collective term for the group of people who cast a show; normally a casting director, director and one or more producers (plus any assistants).

Industry figures/industry professionals: generally refers to non-actor interviewees.

Auditions are sometimes described as castings or meetings (distinct from 'agent meetings').

Wherever possible the advice is tailored to one of three career stages:

1. Final year students on a drama course
2. Actors entering the profession without training or experience
3. Recent grads and other actors in the first years of their career

Working on your career – an overview

'There are so many factors that make the ingredients right for each performer; there is no crystal-ball.' As this experienced agent suggests, there isn't one simple formula for success. The reality of the industry is that actors are reliant on the decision-making of casting directors, agents, directors and producers, as well as many other factors outside of our control.

So, in the day-to-day of your career experienced industry interviewees advise you to take a step back from thinking about the big, abstract goal of 'success'. Instead, identify and work on the things *you can influence* when it comes to getting jobs and staying afloat, and leave the rest – the things you can't control – in the hands of industry figures.

To do this, focus on the quality of your efforts rather than your results. With this attitude, success becomes more about 'What can I improve about the way I prepare for auditions?' rather than 'Did I get the part?'; 'Am I doing the right things to get me through this period of unemployment?' rather than 'When is this going to end?'; and 'I can relax and really enjoy this job' rather than 'What work will it lead to next?'

As one agent explains, 'you shouldn't try to control and worry about something that is inevitably out of your hands; what type of opportunities you'll get and when they'll come. By focusing on and worrying about those, you detract from your ability to take those opportunities.'

This sort of mindset takes practice to get into. But if you can slowly shift your attention away from success in conventional terms – from the end-goal – you'll be able to put more energy towards the things that actually might lead you there.

Based on the advice of experienced actors and industry professionals, the building blocks of an acting career – the things you can work on – can be grouped into four main areas, covered by the four parts of this guide.

For free resources to help you make the most of the expert advice in this chapter, visit www.actorscareerbible.com/freestuff

Building blocks for working on your career

THE BASICS

Getting the simple stuff in order

Your selling points

Work on:

- Understanding your strengths and areas to improve
- Developing your selling points

Understanding the industry

Work on:

- Researching the industry
- Starting your own mini-industry database
- Focusing in on your most realistic opportunities

Photos, CV, showreels and email

Work on:

- Creating your marketing materials
- Making sure they're easy for industry figures to view and use
- Keeping them updated
- Finding the right time to upgrade
- Smartening up your email

FINDING WORK

Getting the attention of agents and casting teams. Find a balance of methods

Casting sites
Work on:
- Choosing casting sites that suit your career stage and budget
- Using the sites effectively

Direct contact
Work on:
- Understanding the principles behind effective direct contact
- Applying for jobs
- Inviting industry to see your work
- Making the most of other opportunities for emailing

Finding the right agent
Work on:
- Getting everything in place before making approaches
- Creating an effective submission
- Navigating agent meetings
- Handling offers
- Dealing with a 'No' at any point

Building your relationship with your agent
Work on:
- Communicating effectively with your agent
- Maintaining a useful attitude
- Making yourself easy to promote
- Adopting the right level of self-marketing

Online marketing
Work on:
- Finding the right options for you
- Building your online presence
- Using online marketing for research and finding opportunities

Networking
Work on:
- Understanding the basics of networking
- Finding opportunities
- Using your network

AUDITIONING

Making the most of opportunities

Preparing for auditions
Work on:
- Prioritizing what to prepare
- Improving each element of how you prepare

On the day
Work on:
- Using the hours before an audition
- Avoiding common mistakes in the room
- Keeping a level head afterwards
- Picking out lessons to learn for next time

Self-taping
Work on:
- Experimenting with your set-up and becoming comfortable with each aspect of the process
- Familiarizing yourself with other self-taping options

UNEMPLOYMENT AND MONEY

Making quiet periods bearable and productive . . . now and for the long term

Dealing with unemployment
Work on:
- Keeping yourself mentally buoyant
- Staying afloat financially
- Giving yourself the best chance of getting back into acting work

Tax and self-employment
Work on:
- Understanding the basics
- Knowing what to do, when

Prioritizing what to work on

Like many of the actors I spoke to for this guide, you might not be exactly sure where to start when it comes to working on your career. If that's the case, the flow charts in this section will help you prioritize. They are based on industry advice covering longer-term priorities for each career stage, common short-term aims for actors, as well as some quick-fix ideas to get you on your way.

Long-term aims based on your career stage

What's important for your average final year student isn't necessarily a priority for an actor who's spent half a decade in the profession. Focus your mid- and longer-term efforts on the most important areas for your career stage, and you'll give yourself a better chance of success.

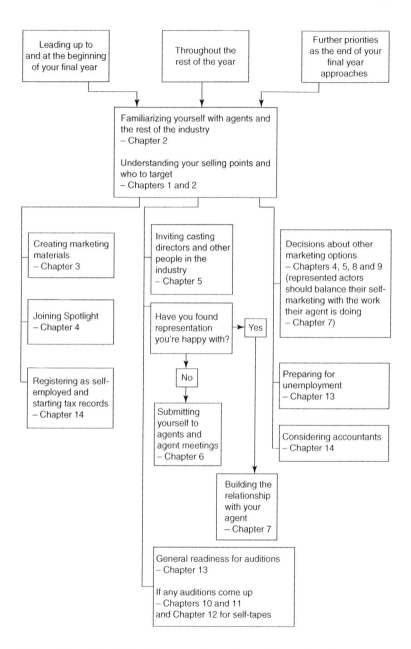

Flow Chart 1: What to work on if you're a final year drama student

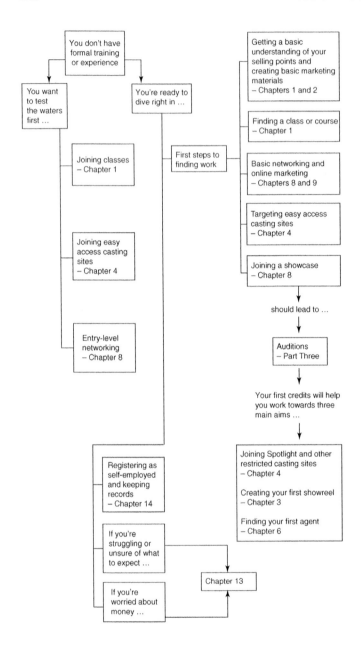

Flow Chart 2: What to work on if you're entering the industry without formal training or experience

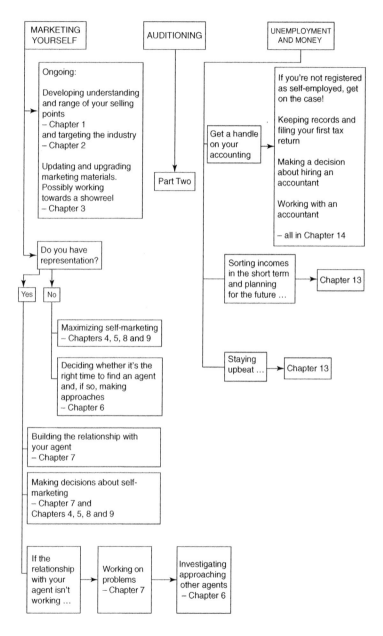

Flow Chart 3: What to work on in the first few years of your career

Continuing through the early part of your career

Some of the actors I spoke to who were further into their careers had felt they'd reached a plateau. They couldn't see a way of landing the credits they needed to attract a new agent, weren't interested in the level of work casting sites could offer and had often become disillusioned with sending out reams of emails to the industry and getting no response. If you're in this situation, the best (and perhaps only!) option is to carefully go through each area of your career and find opportunities for small improvements. There are guidelines on how to do this in each chapter of *The Actor's Career Bible*.

A priority that came up again and again for actors at slightly later career stages is building a lifestyle that works with an acting career. In this case finding the right second job or even second career becomes a high priority, and there's advice on this in Chapter 13.

Priorities based on your immediate situation

Sometimes as an actor you have to forget long-term planning or setting self-help style career goals. Once you've entered the profession, actors interviewed say that immediate priorities will often be determined by your shifting situation: whether you're in acting work or between jobs; you have an audition to prepare or you're waiting for the phone to ring.

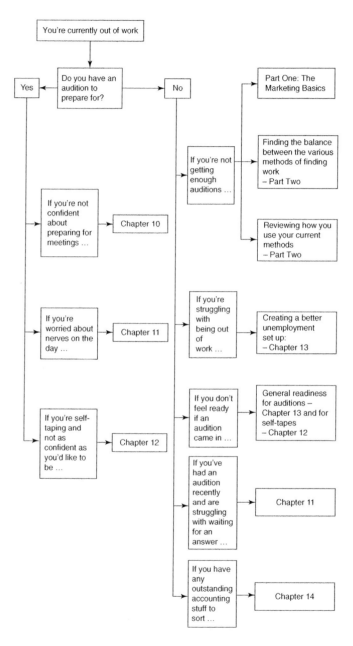

Flow Chart 4: Immediate priorities if you're out of work

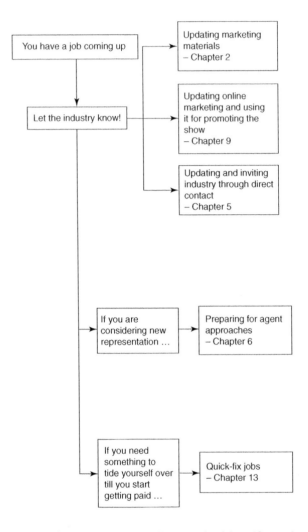

Flow Chart 5: Immediate priorities if you've got a job coming up

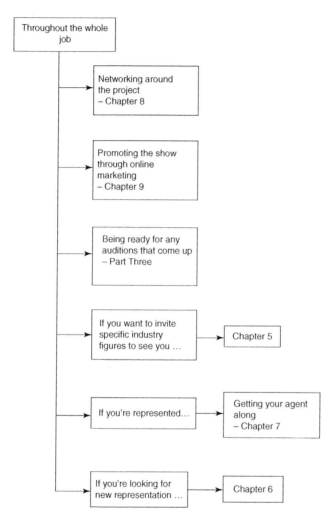

Flow Chart 6: Immediate priorities if you're on a job

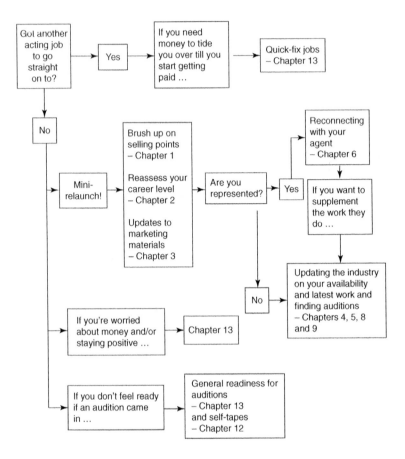

Flow Chart 7: Extra priorities if you're coming to the end of an acting job

If you are still not sure where to start . . .

If after all that you're still struggling to know where to begin, don't worry. Many actors I spoke to took a pretty relaxed attitude to planning how they work on their career. Sometimes simplifying everything is the best approach.

Some I spoke to prioritized an area to work on based on what they enjoyed (or could be bothered to do). Let's face it, at times working on your career can be dull, time-consuming and frustrating: no-one

I spoke to was excited by the idea of emailing a load of agents or searching for an accountant. However, many actors loved the thought of starting their own projects or going to see a load more theatre. While the boring stuff is important, if you're struggling to get yourself going then start with the one thing you might enjoy and have enough motivation to see through.

Alternatively, if you feel like you've got loads of energy to throw at your career or you want something to galvanize you, pick an area you find challenging and set yourself an ambitious target to go after. One actor I spoke to decided they wanted to land a new agent within six months. Whether they achieved this goal or not, the fact it put them in to some sort of action was useful for their career.

Another way to prioritize is by picking an area you've neglected or avoided. For example, you may never have really got into online marketing, been to classes or signed up to a casting site. You might have a really good reason why, but if not, investigate exploring new options.

You could even pick an area at random. It's such an unpredictable industry that this kind of approach can make sense. No one can guarantee what will work for you so pick something on a whim and just get going.

Finally, if you want the simplest approach, plan to do nothing. Part of the point of planning what you work on is that it gives you a sense of control in an industry where footholds are hard to come by, and deliberately making the choice to do nothing in particular towards your career for a while is still a choice. Actors I interviewed came up with lots of good reasons to do nothing; for example, if things are going particularly well, if you're feeling a bit frazzled from struggling or because there just isn't anything obvious that can be done to help you right now. In these cases, sometimes waiting for a change can be better than forcing things.

For free resources to help you make the most of the expert advice in this chapter, visit www.actorscareerbible.com/freestuff

PART ONE
THE BASICS

1
YOUR SELLING POINTS

'Selling points' is a term used to describe the various strengths of an actor, and they are what agents and casting teams assess when deciding who to represent, audition or employ. Understand your own strengths and you'll be able to promote yourself more effectively – as one top agent advises, 'know what your product is, and play to it'. Develop those strengths and work on your weaknesses, and you'll make yourself more employable in the eyes of casting teams and agents.

Use the advice in this chapter to work on:

- Understanding your strengths and areas to improve
- Developing your selling points

Assessing and working on your selling points

It is not just about your talent, it's about you as a product. The more you can be in charge of your product, the faster things can move.
British actor working in Hollywood

The following pages outline a range of selling points suggested by interviewees. To begin working on your own selling points, go through the list, noting down the following:

1   Your current strengths

2   Any weaknesses (areas you could potentially improve)

3   Initial thoughts on what to work on

There is an example on pages 13 and 14 of what this initial assessment might look like. You can revisit your assessment of your selling points as your career develops.

Skills

Note down any skills you have, and to what level (if in doubt, think in terms of basic, intermediate or advanced). Among actors interviewed, examples include singing ability, dancing, driving a vehicle, sporting prowess, horse riding, martial arts training, acrobatics training, circus training, languages, musical ability and stage combat qualifications.

Improving your skills

Most of us have only so much time and money to work on skills, so interviewees suggest ways to prioritize. Start by improving anything you already have at a basic level, or that's a bit rusty (a recent graduate told me, 'a casting director isn't always going to go to Paris to find a French person; they'll cast the French-speaking guy in London. I polished up, got it on my CV and asked my agent to push for those auditions'). Then look at casting breakdowns to find skills commonly called for. For example, a stage actor I spoke to opened up more castings by working on their singing; another actor getting regular commercial auditions was learning to drive. Finally, take up anything else you have an interest in and once you're vaguely competent, get it on your CV.

Accents

Note down any accents you already have some experience with and assess how audition-ready they are. Based on the expectations of casting directors I spoke to, a typical list of accents for actors at early career stages includes: the actor's native accent; RP (Received Pronunciation); general American (seen as a key selling point for anyone regularly auditioning for screen work); and a few other general UK accents.

Working on your accents

There are several ways actors suggest you can make your accents more of a strength:

- Maintain and improve any accents you have already learnt

- Work on accents that could come up for you because of your look or family ties. For example, if you've got a typically Scandinavian look then you could get seen for characters from that region; or if one of your parents grew up in Germany that could get you in the casting room for a German accent role

- Once you've got the most common ones sewn up you can choose to keep working on any UK or world accents you think might be useful

- Buy or set up whatever methods you need to work on accents at short notice for auditions (see list below)

For focused work on accents, actors recommended:

- Books and CD series such as the Access Accents range

- Online sites like International Dialects of English Archive (google 'IDEA accents'), apps such as The Accent Kit and through YouTube (e.g. more than one actor I spoke to recommended 'Rachel's English' for the American accent)

- Private lessons with a dialect coach. Contact ex-teachers and dialect coaches you've worked with on jobs, look through the *Actors and Performers Yearbook* and ask other actors for recommendations

- Calling up a friend with that accent and asking them for help; especially useful for last-minute audition-panics

Working on more general aspects of your ability

It isn't easy to be objective about your own ability, so experienced actors suggest instead looking for strengths and weaknesses based on how *confident* you feel in certain areas. Are there mediums or genres you feel more or less comfortable working in? Do you struggle with aspects of the audition process, or self-taping? And does your confidence go through dips? A seasoned performer explains, 'if you are working semi-regularly, then you are flexing the acting muscles. But if you've been out of work for a long time, you can think, "Christ Almighty, I haven't spoken in front of an audience for a year … what if I get an audition?!"'

Ongoing training is encouraged for all but the most busy and confident actors, with one career coach saying, 'you'll be match-fit, mentally strong and engaged in the industry'. There is a wide range of options:

- Professional training centres such as the Actor's Centre and organizations such as the Actors' Guild

- Workshops run by theatre companies; check the websites of any you're interested in

- Summer schools and short courses run by drama schools

- Graduate classes run by your drama school

- One-on-one coaching

- Train with friends. For example, a recent graduate says this can be a fun and easy way to get a bit of performing-practice in: 'I don't do a lot; I just have a friend who I read through plays with in my spare time. Any play we have an interest in, we'll get together and read all the parts. It keeps my confidence going'

- A DIY approach. Actor-interviewees suggest you can work on anything from stretching and yoga to practising self-taping

Your credits

The amount of work you've done, the regularity, the type and the level are all part of your selling points and affect which roles you're seen for.

An important note: if you don't yet have a long list or wide range of credits to assess, don't worry. Several casting directors and agents point out that's exactly what they expect from actors at the beginning of their careers, and there are opportunities for actors at all levels. And, as one experienced agent explains, 'there are some actors who have done nothing, the right role fits and they land it; there is no way of predicting that'.

To make a start, look at the strengths of individual credits, professionally or while training:

- The director, writer, producer/s and actors you've worked with. Are they prestigious, well-respected, award-nominated/winning, established or up-and-coming?

- The venues and production companies you've worked for: what impressive stuff can you pick out?

- The roles you've played: a lead, co-lead, guest-lead, supporting role, all of which can be selling points. Any size role in a project at a higher level than you normally work is also worth noting down on your list of strengths

The second thing you're looking for are patterns over your whole list of credits: individuals and companies you've worked with more than once; genres (such as comedy or period drama) or mediums (TV, film, theatre) that you've worked in repeatedly; and even the simple fact that you've worked relatively regularly is a selling point.

Applying the same idea, look for areas of weakness (and therefore opportunity!): for example, that you have a lot of theatre credits but not much yet on-screen.

Developing your credits as a selling point

The rest of this guide is designed to give you more control over the shape of your career, and the next chapter goes into further detail about how to assess your credits and begin targeting specific areas of the industry for work.

Profile level

'Profile' refers to how well known an actor is by audiences and people in the industry, and the type and quality of work they are known for. As one producer describes, 'it's a sad reality of the industry but thinking as a producer, if I've got somebody well known, more people will come to see the show and I'm more likely to get press coverage'.

If you're like most actors at early career stages, then this isn't going to be a huge selling point for you yet. Even so, it's worth assessing whether you have the right marketing in place to build a profile over the coming years of your career. Are you promoting the acting jobs you get at this early stage? Are you easy to find and contact online? And are you out and about meeting people in the industry (networking)?

Training and education

While many well-known actors have had success without any form of training, if you have completed a course then this can be a strength in the eyes of agents and casting teams, with one top agent saying, 'as a recent graduate, a high-quality training can help you get seen for lots of jobs'.

You don't have to have formal training, however, to make use of this selling point. One casting director I spoke to says you can 'put a great coach you've worked with on your CV', while several non-drama school actors interviewed list reputable short courses they've done. Even non-acting education can be a selling point. Universities with a history of performers going straight into the profession can carry cachet (Oxford and Cambridge being the most obvious examples), and for some actors I spoke to this has been worth advertising. A few actor-interviewees who'd studied non-acting subjects use their interesting degrees as a selling point, either because their degree is related to something called for in a part or simply as a talking point at auditions or agent meetings.

For a clearer sense of how training is generally perceived by casting teams and agents, ask for opinions from people you trust associated with the profession. If you want to go further, compare the credits and representation of a range of graduates from your course with those from other courses.

The way you work

'People want to work with nice, hard-working professional actors who get the job done brilliantly,' says a leading agent, one of several industry figures who emphasize the importance of actors' behaviour on set and in a rehearsal room. Another agent I spoke to describes the value of general 'enthusiasm, confidence and positivity. A good attitude towards the industry is one of your weapons [which] you need to take into meetings.' Weariness, anxiety and complaining about your lot are seen as off-putting in professional situations, with our agent-interviewee adding, 'the industry just is the way it is. You either embrace it or opt out.'

Casting directors meanwhile reveal that part of their job is matching an actor's personality to suit a director's working style. Some directors will prefer a more formal relationship with their cast, others a bit more relaxed and matey. As one theatre director notes, 'if I'm going to be working with you for twelve weeks I probably want to spend time thinking about what kind of person you are'.

This is another selling point that's difficult to be objective about, so experienced actors suggest thinking about the basics: do you turn up on time, prepare well, display confidence and comfort in audition rooms and on jobs, and not cause unnecessary fuss? A good reputation can get you re-employed by directors, brought back again and again to audition by casting directors and increase your chances of being recommended to others in the industry. A bad reputation can have just as big an effect. As another top agent warns, 'you will quickly learn if you haven't got it right'.

Developing this selling point

If you are concerned you might not be getting it right then focus on the basics listed above. Beyond that, Part Three of this guide will help you impress at auditions and Chapter 8 has tips on how to get more involved in the industry and build your understanding of how the profession works. And while as many interviewees highlight, some negativity from time to time in a tricky profession is totally natural, the time to address this is if your mood is consistently being affected. If you see auditioning as a trial by fire then go to Part Three of this guide; and go to Chapter 13 to improve your mood during periods out of work.

The reputation of your agent

If your agent is known for having great clients or being easy to work with, then, as one casting director put it, this can act as a kind of 'stamp of quality'. While nothing's guaranteed, in theory having a more reputable agent will improve your chances of landing more (and higher-level) auditions. Some actors I spoke to also find their agency's name lends legitimacy to their self-marketing efforts.

Every actor I spoke to had some sense of how agents' reputations differ. It's important to remember that despite this, any perceived hierarchy isn't set in stone; actors from all sorts of agencies work on all sorts of jobs. For a clearer idea of various agents' general reputations, talk to more experienced performers, look up which actors are represented by which agents and browse through agency websites.

Making more of the reputation of your agent

Include your agent's name and branding in your self-marketing: for example, your Twitter bio or website. A bigger step is to look for new representation; if you're considering this, go to Chapter 6 for advice.

Your general presentation

'You're in one of the few industries where you are the product you're selling ... don't go around looking shoddy!' As this agent suggests, your general presentation will make an impression at auditions, agent meetings and even when bumping into industry-people out and about.

The advice here is largely common sense: don't turn up anywhere you might meet people from the industry unwashed, hung-over, exhausted or dressed in rags. Chapters 6, 8, 10 and 11 have further advice if you're unsure what to wear and how to present yourself at agent meetings, networking events and auditions.

Industry knowledge as a selling point

'Knowledge about the industry shows you're passionate and is reassuring and attractive; you seem like the real deal,' an agent explains. Be aware of what's happening on a larger scale (such as who's winning awards, who's starring in TV dramas, what's on at the big theatres) and what's happening around your career level (i.e. projects you have the most realistic chance of working on, based on your credits, training and other strengths). If you're working towards a specific goal (e.g. trying to get the attention of a particular casting director or agent) then you may need to put some time in; otherwise keeping up to date can be as easy as occasionally flicking through Twitter or chatting to mates in the profession.

Confidence with marketing yourself

A few of the agents I spoke to mentioned that confidence with self-marketing (using direct contact, networking and online marketing effectively) is attractive in actors they're considering for representation. As one explained, 'that work ethic is a sign you're not expecting an agent to do it all for you, and that you take your career seriously'. Equally, over-marketing or being too pushy is often cited as 'a big no-no', as one casting director put it. Use the rest of Parts One and Two of this guide to get the balance right.

Understanding your casting

Your 'casting' is a description of the characters industry figures think you could play, mainly based on your look, personality and acting skills. This section lists the most common casting categories that came up during interviews.

At early career stages, aim for an awareness of your main casting type/s. As one recent graduate has found, it's useful 'to fit at least one easily identifiable bracket so that people have a basis from where to cast you'. As your career develops, you should be able to get a more developed sense of how you're seen by casting teams.

Some areas are more subjective (you might not be 100 per cent sure if casting directors see you as 'enigmatic'). For those categories, keep your ideas sensible, simple and open to change, with casting directors warning you can limit yourself if you come up with too complicated or firm an idea of what you could or couldn't be cast as. Interviewees suggest two ways to find extra clues about your casting (you're after patterns that suggest how you're seen generally): asking for opinions from people you trust in the industry and looking at breakdowns of roles you've been called in for.

The advice in the rest of this guide will show you how to highlight your casting by making very clear choices with your marketing. As with other selling points, you can also work on expanding your range. The actors I interviewed suggest three main ways to do this: changing your look (for example, some actors got a new hairstyle; others spent time in the gym); tweaking photos, CVs and showreels to show off more range;

and working on areas of your acting to improve your range of characters and comfort in different styles and mediums (see pages 5 and 6).

Physical characteristics

Casting teams will often be looking for certain physical types, so your height, build, hair colour, hairstyle/length and even eye colour can be a decision point. Anything definable can be useful for getting the attention of agents and casting teams; for example, one actor told me that 'my curly hair seems to make me stand out from the crowd'. Anything unusual will help you get seen for niche casting; for example, actors I spoke to make a selling point out of being especially tall or short, hugely muscly or very slim.

Playing age

The ages you could convincingly play. For Spotlight it is normally a ten-year span. Other casting sites use a smaller range or even a single number. Casting directors explain that on-screen, most actors will have smaller range usually close to their age; for theatre it's generally easier to be convincing as a younger or older person.

Nationality, ethnicity and geographical ties

Some projects will look for actors of a certain ethnicity or for actors from (or with an affiliation to) a particular country or region. One actor with heritage from different parts of the world describes their casting: 'I've played British parts, but I've been cast in Asian, Mediterranean and French roles.'

Consider your look and the regions that links you to; where you were born and grew up; where your close family members are from; and any languages or accents you've picked up that could link you to a country or area.

Characteristics and character types

Casting directors recommend you think about characteristics and character types suggested by your physical characteristics, your personality and those you find easy to adopt in performance.

Characteristics mentioned by actors, casting teams and agents during interviews include qualities like 'elegance', 'mischief', 'intelligence', 'warmth', 'confidence', 'edginess', 'toughness', 'nerviness', 'polite-ness', 'innocence', 'coldness', 'high energy' and 'low tempo'.

Casting teams and actors also talk about stock character types: for example, sporty, romantic lead, girl/boy next door, the fool, leaders, heroines/heroes, loveable losers, geeks, everyman/woman. Sometimes character types are also based on class or a job.

Genre, style and medium

Some actors told me that casting directors seem to associate them with a particular genre (e.g. comedy or period drama) or medium (they are known more for stage than screen work or vice versa). If you've been in the industry for a while, look at your previous credits to see if there is anything particular you're associated with.

Example list of selling points

What do they see … what sells you?

Experienced agent

The example below is for a final year drama student, based on a range of interviewees' experiences. It will give you a good idea of what an initial assessment of your strengths, weaknesses and plans to improve might look like.

Rosa is a term away from entering the profession. She makes a list of her current selling points, which include:

- General ability: very comfortable performing on stage
- Skills: a good range, including songs she can use for auditions, three sports to a high level, guitar to a good standard, a high-level second language
- Accents: confident in RP, general American, other regional accents learnt on the course, and Spanish
- Previous credits: played several interesting roles and worked with two well-known directors in that time
- Training and education: graduating from a well-known drama school

- Personality/mood: ongoing interest from agents has given her confidence, and she's excited to get out into the profession

Rosa then assesses her casting:

- Average height, dark eyes and medium length dark curly hair
- Playing age is 15–25
- Close family links to Southern Spain and can speak the language
- Has played a range of interesting character parts
- Based on all this Rosa decides her most obvious casting niche is Mediterranean roles and characters from Spanish-speaking countries

Having made this assessment, Rosa decides she wants to improve in two main areas before she enters the industry: confidence with screen performance (general acting ability) and to broaden her understanding of the characteristics and character types she might be seen for. She begins by working on self-taping with her screen-acting teacher and asks staff to help her clarify her potential casting.

For free resources to help you make the most of the expert advice in this chapter, visit www.actorscareerbible.com/freestuff

2
UNDERSTANDING THE INDUSTRY

This chapter lays out how to source and keep track of industry information, vital for almost every aspect of an actor's efforts to promote themselves. The final part of this chapter takes you through two ways of narrowing down the huge number of agents and casting teams out there, so you can begin focusing on your most realistic opportunities for work.

Use the advice in this chapter to work on:

- Finding useful information about the industry
- Starting your own mini-industry database
- Focusing in on your most realistic opportunities

Researching the industry

Get digging ... work out what's out there.

Successful screen actor

If you're about to enter the profession, one of your first aims should be to familiarize yourself with who's who and what's what. Once you're in the industry proper, being able to find good information will be useful for developing almost every aspect of your career.

You'll pick up all sorts of industry info through social media, talking with friends and contacts, reading and watching as much as you can, and even through simple Google searches. This first section in this chapter will guide you through the other main industry information sources actors use and what to look out for.

Where to look

- The IMDb (Internet Movie Database) website. The free version is useful for finding out about actors and casting teams' previous work. The subscription version (IMDb Pro) gives more detailed information, including contact details (Chapter 10 covers advice on when it's worth paying for the Pro version)
- The Casting Director's Guild website
- The Personal Manager's Association website
- Casting directors', producers', directors' and writers' personal sites
- Agency websites
- Actors' personal websites
- Theatre venue/company websites
- Film and TV production company websites
- Email and mailing lists of theatres and production companies
- Listings guides: for example, the *Actors and Performers Yearbook* and *Contacts*
- Industry news sites: for example, The Stage, WhatsOnStage
- Career advice on sites like Act On This, Spotlight and Equity
- Industry-related podcasts, such as The Spotlight podcast, The Honest Actors' Podcast, The 98% podcast, The Two Shot Podcast
- Casting sites (some offer industry newsletters and directories)
- Spotlight search; a simple way to find out who an actor is represented by
- Reviews of productions online and in newspapers (e.g. Theatre Record)

What to look out for

Agents

- The type and level of work their clients are doing
- Patterns in their list: for example, if they represent lots of actor-singers
- Gaps on their list
- Names of associates and assistants
- Contact details
- Information about how they prefer to be contacted

Casting directors, producers, directors and writers

- The medium and genres they tend to work in
- Who they regularly work with: venues/companies; other casting directors/producers/directors/writers; their assistants and associates
- The previous experience of actors they tend to cast
- Any links you can find with them; for example, if you know they've seen your work, you've seen projects they've worked on, or there are actors or other people in the industry you've both worked with or know
- Contact details
- How open they are to being contacted directly and which contact methods they prefer
- Any advice on what to include when contacting them … and what to avoid

Theatre, film and TV

- Theatre production companies/venues, and TV and film production companies: the type of work they do; whether they cast in-house or regularly use particular casting directors; the regular producers, directors and writers they work with

- The level of actor they usually work with (look at different-size roles). What kind of experience, representation and other selling points do the actors have? Where do you fit in at this stage of your career?
- Any contact details and preferences

Other actors

- Look at other actors' credits: the venues/companies they've worked for; the casting teams they've worked with
- Who they're represented by
- Their marketing, for instance: do they have a website? what type of showreel and photos do they use? how do they use social media?

Maintaining your own mini-industry database

Get a spreadsheet of casting directors and their contact details, and keep track of your communication. This is key!

Actor, over fifteen years' experience in the profession

The super-organized actors I spoke to keep an ongoing record of the industry information they come across: useful for finding an agent, direct contact, networking and auditioning. You can start by listing your current contacts. As you work through this guide and move through your career, add to your lists and build up your database. Actors say that even jotting down a few notes every so often will benefit you in the long term, but if you want a more methodical approach then follow the example of one performer who told me, 'I have three databases and each has various sub groups!' Using a spreadsheet or table:

- List agents, casting directors, producers, directors, writers, venues and production companies, actors and other contacts
- Categorize them (or have separate databases): for example, casting directors all together, then agents, etc.; separate those

that are realistically worth targeting for work and those at the next levels up; or those you've already met, and those you want to meet next

- Include details about their work: for example, mediums, genres, regular collaborators

- Keep a note of any interactions: for example, when you've contacted them, responses you've received, when you've auditioned for them, projects of theirs you've seen, when they've seen your work and any mutual contacts you have

- Jot down any contact details you can find and any information on how they prefer to be contacted

Example

Currently targeting

Name	Type of work	Contact/interaction/links	Contact details
Agents/agencies			
Miller Management	Takes on lots of graduates	Emailed showreel 11/17 (reply asking to email back when next in something)	sarah@mmcasting
Mark Willburn	Mainly Musical Theatre actors	Saw my showcase	Ask John F to pass on email to me
Casting directors			
Jenny H Casting	Theatre, mainly tours	Saw me on Hedda tour	jenny@jennyh.com
Slam Casting	TV comedy	Came to talk to us at drama school	Website here

Focusing in on your most realistic opportunities

Occasionally I take a stab in the dark, but usually I will see people I've seen perform, or I've seen their showreel, or they're represented

*by someone I know has good taste, or have been to a drama school
that is of a standard.*

Experienced TV casting director

It's easy to get fixated on agents and jobs several steps ahead of you
but, as the quote above suggests, being realistic is important if you
want to regularly get seen. Identify the casting teams and agents most
likely to be interested in what you currently offer, and you'll not only
increase your chances of getting meetings, you'll also give yourself a
clear direction for your marketing and a manageable workload (as one
recent graduate describes, the size of the industry 'can be overwhelm-
ing, and it's easy to do the ostrich thing and just dunk your head in the
sand').

Interviewees suggest two simple ways to build up a picture of what's
currently most realistic. The first is to search for opportunities based
on your selling points. Here's two examples, based on suggestions by
actors, using previous credits as a starting point:

1 Pick out a director you've worked with, either while training or
   professionally, and (using the sources on page 16) to find out
   what they've been working on recently and what they're doing
   next. This may well reveal a job you could apply for, but you'll
   almost certainly come across casting directors, producers and
   companies they're linked to, each of which could be worth targeting. You'll also find out which actors that director has cast
   recently. If one or two have a similar level of experience to you,
   look at other projects they've been working on and the casting
   teams involved.

2 Look up actors you've recently performed with. If they've played
   a similar size role to you, their list of credits will throw up names
   and companies to keep track of and target in the future. If a fellow actor is further into their career, their CV will give you a sense
   of trajectory and the kind of credits to target to move towards
   that level.

Apply this process to your other selling points, looking out for casting
teams and agents to target. For instance, if you're represented, look at
the client lists of agents with a similar reputation to yours. If you're training, look through recent graduates' credits. And if you have particular

skills and accents, search for projects and casting teams that regularly require them. Do the same with your casting types; for example, if your look suggests characters from a certain region, search for companies or writers with that focus.

The second way to narrow down the industry is to use a checklist to decide if opportunities you come across are worth pursuing. For specific jobs, casting directors advise checking:

- You meet the basic casting criteria (you're in roughly the right age and look brackets)
- You have some relevant training or credits
- You can perform the skills or accents required

If you're ticking these boxes then you can be confident it's worth applying or making a suggestion to your agent. But your chances will be boosted if you also have:

- A link to the script (e.g. it's set where you grew up, or you simply have a passion for that particular story – 'follow your interests', encourages one successful performer)
- A link with the casting team (e.g. you've worked with the director previously, or you know the casting director has seen you perform)

You can use a similar checklist to be more targeted with all your marketing efforts. For example, if you're considering inviting a casting director to see your show or deciding if it's worth keeping tabs on a theatre company, ask yourself if you have the right experience and skills or a link to the person/company's projects.

While one casting director advises 'tick as many boxes as you can', they add that sometimes there are 'unusual circumstances'; if you have a niche casting type or offer rare skills, then a lack of experience may not be a problem. The same applies the other way around; if you're offering a bit of profile or a lot of experience, then the casting team may be more flexible with the casting type they're looking for.

All this doesn't mean you can't take the odd shot in the dark. But thinking carefully about opportunities before you apply will up your chances and prevent you pestering, with casting teams and agents interviewed saying actors who pay attention to these details make a much better impression.

For free resources to help you make the most of the expert advice in this chapter, visit www.actorscareerbible.com/freestuff

3
PHOTOS, CVS, SHOWREELS AND EMAIL

Photos, CVs and showreels advertise your strengths – or 'selling points' – to the industry. To enter the profession you only need simple headshots and a basic CV, but as your career continues you can build up a package buying new photos, updating your CVs and creating showreels. Meanwhile, there are some simple things you can do to professionalize your email, so you make a good impression whenever you contact the industry.

Use the advice in this chapter to work on:

- Creating your marketing materials
- Making sure they're easy to view and use
- Keeping them updated
- Finding the right time to upgrade
- Smartening up your email

Creating a portfolio of versatile headshots

Be methodical. Research. Make a short-list. Budget ... then go with your gut!

Member of the Association of Professional Headshot
Photographers (APHP)

The standard headshot – the style that most UK casting directors and agents will expect – is a head and shoulders photo, with you looking directly into the camera. Colour is now used almost universally but industry figures still recommend you have a black-and-white version of at least one of your photos. While most of your headshots will be portrait, 'one of the current trends is to have a landscape shot', a photographer explains. 'They're good for general marketing; film and TV are landscape so the headshot looks more like it's been dragged out of the screen.' A few actors I spoke to also have mid- or full-length body shots. According to casting directors, for most actors this is not necessary; by showing the shoulders the standard headshot gives enough sense of an actor's body-shape.

Rather than aiming for a single perfect photo, professional photographers will help you to create a 'portfolio', normally made up of three to five headshots. As one explains, 'you're aiming to portray all the roles you want to do in as few shots as possible, and, while you can have more, three photos is normally enough'. Anyone looking at your portfolio will then quickly get an idea of your range, and you (and your agent if you're represented) have options when submitting for auditions.

When to get headshots

If you're a drama student, your course staff will advise you when to get your first headshots. If it's not timetabled for you, or if you're entering the profession via another route, make booking a session a priority.

For many actors I spoke to, their first set served them well for at least their first year or two in the profession. A few actors warn that upon signing with agents, you may be asked to get a new set – a touch annoying if you've just spent around £350. Unfortunately, there's not much you can do about this; you'll need headshots to get an agent's attention in the first place, and agents point out they have to be happy with the shots they're promoting you with.

If you're represented and considering getting new shots then discuss your reasons with your agent. Otherwise, there are a couple of traps to avoid when it comes to updating your photos. As one actor describes, 'getting new pictures can often feel like the solution when you're feeling stressed and things aren't going well', but this isn't always a great strategy; your photos may not be the problem and you can end up wasting money getting rid of perfectly good shots. On the other hand, another actor highlights that as you get older, 'the risks of clinging on too long are much bigger than the financial risk of changing them too soon'.

To guard against these problems, interviewees suggest two good reasons for changing your headshots in your early years in the profession:

1   If your photos don't reflect your main casting types. Almost every industry figure I spoke to about this says that at least one of your shots should be close to the natural, everyday you that walks into the casting room, and the rest of your portfolio should represent your other major casting brackets.

2   If your photos, as one leading photographer explains, aren't 'high quality' and don't 'reflect the latest headshot trends'. To get a sense of what you should be aiming for, ask for a range of opinions from people you're close to in the industry, and look at shots of other actors on photographer galleries or leading agency websites (ignore any superstar actors with arty photos) to see if yours is badly taken or edited, or the style is out of date.

Finding your photographer

If you've made the decision to get new photos, the next step is to find the right photographer. The most basic requirement is that they're a professional specialist in actors' headshots; don't just use a mate who happens to have a camera.

Many actors I spoke to found their photographer through recommendations, usually straight from actor-friends. One photographer suggests 'you can find people through asking on Facebook and Twitter, and if you hear a photographer's name you can check them out on Instagram'. Students can get recommendations from their course staff, and if you're represented speak to your agent.

Actors and photographers offer lots of ideas on how to widen your search. A great place to start is the Association of Professional Headshot Photographers website (aphp.co.uk). You can find even more in listing guides like the *Actors and Performers Yearbook*, and agency and drama school websites with photo-galleries of their actors are another good place to search. You can also try the IMDb website (imdb.com). The advance search function allows you to narrow things down to people with a similar playing age to you; and if you have an IMDb Pro subscription you can even search for actors with a similar look. Beyond that, Google is your friend here: type in 'headshot photographers' and a host of websites will come up.

Photographers suggest you can make your final decision based simply on your gut reaction; if you like someone's photos and can afford a session then that can be enough. If you're agonizing over several photographers you like, focus on these two questions:

1) Whose style suits you best?

A headshot specialist explains that 'different photographers offer different lighting and looks and their direction will stimulate different results'. As you view each photographer's gallery, look out for their use of lighting and shade, how bright or muted the colours are, the level of retouching, camera position and frame size, how much and which parts of the actor are in focus and the type of backgrounds. You'll soon begin to see how photographers' styles vary: for example, whether shots are glossy or muted; glamorized or more everyday; brightly coloured or more sober; angular or soft; shadowy or light; intense or airy; elegant or gritty; modern and arty or simple and traditional.

Once you have an idea of the various styles, you can then decide which is likely to best suit you. The first key bit of advice here comes from one top agent who says, '(actors) can get away with murder the more well-known they get. But if you are at the beginning of your career, keep it simple. You haven't got the right to start being all fancy and artistic.'

Beyond that, one of your aims, as a photographer explains, 'is to see who offers you the casting types you want to be going for'. Their advice is to think in fairly broad terms. So, if you're predominantly after something that shows you as 'the villain' then a photographer with an angular, shadowy, muted style would be a good choice. But if the main casting you're after is 'the girl/guy next door' go for a photographer who can capture an everyday, brightly coloured, soft and light style. You can apply the same kind of thinking if you're specifically targeting particular genres or mediums. For example, TV roles generally suit a more modern, colourful, glossy style of photo than you would use for targeting straight theatre work. And if you're aiming to target a particular range of agents, look for the photographers their clients use, and any common style elements you can pick out from actors' shots around your age and career-stage.

2) Who can you afford?

A standard-length session can cost anything from £100 to £500. An experienced photographer explains that most headshot specialists are priced in the middle of that bracket, guaranteeing you someone 'good, experienced and a specialist'. Cheaper standard prices (up to £150) will often indicate someone who 'has recently started photographing actors and is on the up. If you like their photos, then they might be great for you and you'll have saved some money.' Prices at the top end can mean you get 'more expertise and experience, or someone who shoots great photos more regularly'. They may be able to charge more because they're constantly in demand or 'you may simply be paying extra for their name and brand'.

Another photographer I spoke to says, 'ideally you'd look at what you want and go for the photographer who can do that, even if they're a bit more money. If someone's £300, you like their work, they're busy, you see their actors on the TV and on stage a lot then I think it's going to be worth it, rather than paying £150 just because someone else is cheaper.' To keep costs down look out for discounts, seasonal and introductory offers. Check photographers' websites, their social media feeds, adverts in listing guides and industry websites (e.g. some casting sites offer discounts for members). And while one leading photographer advises you should 'go for the longest session you can afford', you can save money by opting for a shorter, cheaper session that some photographers offer: 'You can still get great shots but you will need to be more focused and know what you want before you go in.'

Preparing for a session

Once you've booked your session, think about any ideas for your shoot that you want to discuss. A photographer explains, 'as much as I can give you advice on the day, it's important that prior to a session you consider what parts you want to be playing', with another revealing, 'there is a lot of passivity from actors about headshots but actually you can get involved'. Suggestions work best, they say, when they're 'brief, flexible and light, an offer you're making to the photographer'.

You should also think about clothing choices: take a range of options from your everyday wardrobe with you. Make sure everything's clean and ironed, and use a suit or dress cover to transport them. Beyond the most simple advice ('select things that make you feel comfortable and that suit you'), photographers offer a few common tips on what to wear:

- To capture the different casting types you're going for, think in terms of 'subtle suggestions' and 'of "looks" rather than different characters'

- 'Block colours work well. [These should be] sympathetic to your skin-tone and go with your eyes and hair. Muted tones are good because the colour won't distract from your face, but it doesn't have to be pastel; sometimes a bright colour can work'

- 'Solid colours are good as long as nothing gets lost in anything else; so if you've got blonde hair, wearing a yellow shirt is not a good idea'

- 'You've got to sell your personality and your body type. It's important therefore to have clothes that show off the neckline: scooped, circle or V-necks, anything that really clings to the body is good'

- 'Use different shapes and textures … layers work well'

- And finally, avoid anything distracting: 'When I look at a headshot I want to look at a person's eyes first. Anything else and the wrong thing has had its attention brought to it'; 'No complicated patterns'; 'Avoid big collars or that's very bulky like a big winter jumper … and anything too fashiony.' The same ideas apply for any jewellery you're considering; keep things simple

If you want to try a range of makeup options you're advised to start with natural choices. Guys can shave mid-shoot for an easy way to get a different look in their portfolio (remember to check with your photographer that you'll have time). Everyone warns against getting a haircut in the days just before the session. You'll want time to get used to it and if you are unhappy it may undermine your confidence or distract you during the shoot. And don't stress too much if you suddenly break out in spots or something else goes wrong on the day. Photographers will use their editing skills to get rid of any blemishes.

If you've no idea what clothing, hair or makeup choices to go for then look at shots of actors with similar casting types, hair colour and style, skin tone and eye colour. You can also ask your photographer for advice in the days beforehand, and, as long as you bring a range of options, they will use their expertise to help you.

Finally, if anything goes wrong in the days before – you get a haircut you hate or you're feeling really grotty – then photographers advise you contact them to rebook.

Working with your photographer during the shoot

Throughout the session your photographer will guide you through different poses and suggest adjustments to your expression and/or thoughts for different casting types. They will also advise you when to change clothes, hair and makeup, and do what they can to help you relax.

Headshot specialists interviewed say it's important for actors to trust their photographer, listen to suggestions and follow their lead. However, as one explains, the session is 'a collaboration between the actor and the photographer; they have to meet in the middle to some degree', with another photographer advising: 'don't rely on us completely; take some responsibility yourself'. Most photographers will invite you to discuss your ideas with them (why you're getting photos and what you want to get out of the shoot), but if not then don't be afraid to bring this up yourself. Throughout the shoot you can make suggestions, check how things are going (some photographers will let you see the photos) and ask for advice.

To help achieve this sense of 'collaboration', one photographer advises you 'go in to the session being open; like you would if you were going for coffee with a new friend. This helps the actor–photographer relationship; being friendly means you can find a genuine reason to smile or connect, rather than just being told to. If you have your guard up and don't take it down things can become very difficult.' They advise remembering that 'you're joining a network of people with a selfless attitude that wants the same as you; you want to get a job, and the photographer wants you to get a job'.

If you are struggling to relax or getting weary, tell the photographer how you're feeling, have a stretch, drink some water, take a break … do whatever you need to do. And if you're distracted or worried about anything (e.g. your hair falling out of place or whether or not you're capturing a particular expression) ask them to keep an eye on it.

Choosing your final shots

After the session you'll be sent your gallery with all your useable shots. You then pick a few to be edited and retouched, and after that you'll get your final photos. Remember, you're aiming to create a portfolio of varied headshots, as described on page 24.

As one top agent told me, 'actors are often the worst judge of their own pictures', so if you're struggling, ask for advice on what will best serve your aims: from your photographer, your agent if you're represented, drama school teachers, actor-friends and any other close industry contacts. Be careful about seeking opinions from people outside of the acting industry. Your family and non-acting friends will possibly pick a photo based on reasons that aren't valid professionally (probably the one where you're smiling nicely).

Making the most of your photos

'Use your portfolio!' urges one industry-leading photographer, and there are several things you can do immediately upon receiving your finished shots:

- If you're represented, send your photos to your agent to check they agree with your choices

- Update any casting sites you're a member of

- Use your portfolio in the rest of your marketing, including your Twitter pic, your website if you have one and IMDb if you have a Pro subscription

- If you're sending out emails to casting directors and others in the industry (direct contact) you can use your photos in the main body of your emails

- Finally, thank the photographer. Beyond sending an email, like their Facebook page, follow them on Twitter and recommend them to other actors

Other types of photos you can use to market yourself

While, as one industry-leading photographer explains, 'the standard head and shoulders front-on photo, for the time being at least, is still the priority and used industry-wide', there are other shots actors can use in the early stages of their career.

Screen and stage production shots

Snapshots of you performing onscreen can be used throughout your online marketing, especially on the IMDb site. Production shots from plays can be included on a website if you have one, Twitter and other social media. You can include production shots on casting sites, though casting directors advise using them sparingly (especially on Spotlight) – only if they show off a major aspect of your casting not already represented by your headshots.

Photos from industry events

There will often be photographers taking shots of actors at events like press nights and award ceremonies. These photos are especially useful for IMDb and can be used throughout your online marketing more generally. If you think you've been snapped at an event, search online and contact the photographer.

Publicity shots

Actors can pay for glossy, stylized, model-esque photos to supplement their headshots. Some of the more experienced actors I spoke to added them to IMDb pages, casting sites and online marketing. For most actors starting out, though, the advice is that these are an unnecessary expense, with industry figures explaining that an actor's career needs to be at a reasonably high level to pull off including publicity shots in their marketing. If you have the money to spare and really think you might benefit, research what other actors around your career-stage are using and discuss it as an option with your agent.

CVs

> *Looking at an actor's CV is like looking at a map of their whole career.*
> TV casting director, thirty years' experience

Casting teams and agents use CVs to understand an actor's casting range and the level of projects they're suitable for. The advice in this section focuses on personalized CVs: a one-pager you put together yourself, making decisions on the layout, content and presentation. It's an alternative if you're not a member of Spotlight, if you want to create a CV for your own website or if you want to customize a CV to highlight particular selling points when applying to agents or casting directors.

Some represented actors I interviewed simply use their agent's version of their CV: a no-fuss option that allows you to take advantage of their branding. You can download a copy and send it out as is, tweak it or use it as a template. If you don't fancy their version or you're unrepresented, then the guidelines here will show you how to create a personalized CV from scratch.

On the following page is a typical example to help you. For further examples, take a look at CVs on agency websites and search for UK actor CVs online. Be wary of copying American CV templates, as there are some important differences.

John Actor

Agency X,
110 London Avenue,
W18 6YV
0208xxxx898

HEADSHOT

Height: 6ft 1"
Playing range: 25–30
Spotlight: 5674-89x0-344x
john actor@me.com

About
John recently graduated from London Drama Training. A native of South East London, he has recently performed at venues around the country with the Touring Company, and was nominated for a Fringe Film Award for his performance in the short film 'The Way'. He can next be seen in Hamlet at the Shakespeare Theatre, till 29th April.

Training
London Drama Training – 3 year BA
Credits while training including Romeo in 'Romeo and Juliet' and Trevor in 'Playing at Home'.

Roles
Theatre

Role	Production	Director	Company	
Osric	Hamlet	Jane Smith	The Shakespeare Co.	2017
Peter	Old Times	Ezra Brown	The Touring Co.	2016

Television

Role	Production	Director	Company	
Mark (guest)	Doctors	Peter Smith	BBC	2017

Film

Role	Production	Director	Company	
Casper	The Way (short)	Chantelle Jones	Nub Films	2016

Awards
Nominated for Fringe Film Award for The Way

Skills
Full drivers licence
Stage combat
Horse-riding (advanced); tennis (advanced); hockey; boxing
French speaker (advanced)

Accents
London (native), RP, Yorkshire, General American, French

Example of a standard CV for an actor at an early career stage

What to include on your personalized CV

- Your name, your agent's and agency name if you're represented and contact details

- Your height and playing age. Casting directors say you only need to include details like build, eye and hair colour if they're important for a part you're applying for

- Your headshot. If you're struggling for space and you've got a photo in the main body of an accompanying email, then you can get away without one

- Your credits, skills and accents. Indicate if your skills are advanced and which accent is native. For skills, you can include further information (e.g. 'represented England U20s'), use the word 'advanced' in brackets or the Spotlight system (a little '*')

- Your training (if you have it). The advice is that this includes not only drama schools but top coaches you've worked with, courses and summer schools

If you have space, you can also choose to include:

- A mini-biography or 'About' section. Use your name in the third person and quickly summarize your main selling points

- Any award wins or nominations you or the projects you've worked on have received

Laying out your CV

The aim when laying out your CV is to highlight your strongest attributes, and the layout shown on page 33 is a good option for many actors at an early career stage, making a feature of your training and putting less focus on a short list of credits. If you are at a stage where you have a good list of credits then a better layout would be to drop the Bio/About section and push your training section below.

Give a title to your training, roles/credits, awards, skills and accent sections. You could also choose to include titles for your 'About' and agent information. Contact details and info about your appearance can be labelled (e.g. Email: janeactor@me.com; Appearance: Height …), though it's not absolutely necessary.

Include headings for your credits ('Film', 'Television' and 'Theatre'). For other categories (radio, workshops, readings, web series, commercials etc.), put them under their own individual headings, or group them together under 'Other credits'. You can use your training credits to bulk out your other sections or include them under a separate heading, 'Credits whilst training'. Casting directors and agents I spoke to say that if you're new to the industry and have a few credits in areas like web series or short film, don't worry about individual headings; just include the information in brackets next to the title of each project.

If you're applying for a job or to a casting director who works in a particular genre, then put the relevant heading highest on the page. If you don't have a specific aim, then, as one top agent advises, 'put your strengths first; if you have an amazing theatre-career then that's your first tab'. Keep the number of columns you use to four or five. If your CV is looking messy, tuck the dates next to the name of the production or the director's name alongside the production company.

Presentation

'Avoid anything over-elaborate; it's tiresome', warns one casting director. Their and others' advice is to make simple presentational choices that emphasize important information and enhance overall clarity. Coloured, italicized, bold and larger fonts can work if used sparingly for titles, for your name or to highlight the most vital selling points. Simple use of shading, coloured borders or lines to separate sections can also look good. Casting directors and agents suggest where possible choosing colours of the brands that are associated with you: for example, your agency or drama school.

Showreels

I watch a showreel and ask myself is this person good and are they right for what I'm looking for?
                                            Screen and stage casting director

A showreel is any video you use to showcase your acting to the industry. Showreels are predominantly used in screen-casting, normally to help casting teams decide which actors to bring in to audition. Theatre casting directors told me they also occasionally refer to them, with one explaining, 'showreels are something I would look at once I'd got down to a reasonable shortlist and only if I was um-ing and ah-ing'. If you're approaching agents (who will always want to see some of your work before they sign you) a reel can be enough to get their interest or back up any work they've already seen you do.

Do you need a showreel?

If you're brand new to the profession then, as one showreel editor says, 'a reel is not an essential', and your first priority should always be headshots. For actors slightly further along who have already sorted photos, rushing things will do you more harm than good, with a director-producer explaining, 'if you've convinced me you're a "Maybe" then all a bad showreel is going to do is convince me you're a "No" '.

However, as long as you achieve an acceptable production quality, the advice suggests you don't need a host of professional credits to create a reel, nor do you need to spend hundreds of pounds. A screen-casting director says that (as long as the production quality of the reel is decent!), 'any sort of showreel is useful for us to reference', while an Off-West-End theatre director reveals, '[the prestige of the footage] doesn't really matter to me; I just want to see what you look like on camera and how you come across'. I spoke to several actors who'd created professional-looking reels with a single scene from decent look-ing short and student films, clips from web series and well-selected snippets from commercials and music videos. You can shoot scenes yourself: write or find scripts and get some friends together from the industry with a bit of know-how and the right equipment; or, if you take care, even shooting a monologue on a phone or laptop, self tape-style, can be used to start you off.

Creating a showreel

There are various ways to create a showreel; use the tips in this section to decide which method would be best for you. While an experienced showreel editor advises, 'go for the best thing you can, given the foot-age you have available and your budget', to help you further, research what's appropriate for your current aims. For example, if you're at a stage where you're approaching agents, look to see if their clients have reels and, if so, the type of footage and quality. The same applies if you're targeting particular casting teams; look at the reels of actors they have recently cast.

Studio-edited reel of your existing footage

You can pay a specialist editor to put together a showreel for you made up of multiple clips from your existing work. The biggest bonus here is, as one editor says, 'a professional has skills your average home-editor won't', with one busy TV actor I spoke to explaining, 'I'm glad I went to (a proper editor) for my first reel. They cut together lots of clips that were not really scenes at all, where there was so little of me in them … and they made it look like the scenes were all about me!'

Depending on who you choose and what you need doing, you could end up paying anything from £80 up to closer towards £400. If you only have a couple of scenes to edit where you're clearly the star of the show then you might need less expertise, and therefore a less expensive option. And if you have some good editing skills then one editor recommends: 'always have a go at editing your reel yourself. You can then take it to an editor who'll tidy it up for you, for a bit less than if you just turned up with a bag saying "Here's my DVDs".'

Assuming you have the budget, choosing a professional editor is recommended if any of these points apply to you:

- You don't have the editing skills or software necessary to make a reel yourself
- You have some of the skills to edit a reel yourself but want the reassurance and extra guidance offered by an editor
- You don't have time to put something together yourself

DIY reel of your existing footage

For several actors I spoke to, putting a reel together themselves was a cheaper and equally effective option. As one showreel editor outlines, 'it's easy to be swept up in other people's showreel that have really cool montages and look incredibly sleek and sexy ... but you can end up paying a studio editor hundreds of pounds and it's not always necessary early on in your career'.

Actors interviewed say that if you have scenes that require a fair amount of editing, you'll need to be confident using software like Adobe Premiere or Final Cut. But even if your editing skills and software are pretty basic then a home-edited reel is still an option. An editor explains, 'if you're featured as the main character in a couple of good scenes then take those, put a little fade-to-black between each one, stick your name in white font at the front for two seconds and your agent's (or your) contact details at the end for two seconds, and you've got everything a casting director wants from a showreel ... that's something you can do in iMovie so easily'.

DIYing your reel could be a good option for you if any of these points apply:

- You have the skills and software to create a reel yourself
- Your scene/s don't need any editing, and you have the confidence to string them together on iMovie or other simple software
- You want a temporary basic reel before saving up for an editor or while you wait for footage to be released
- You want to try creating your reel yourself before approaching an editor in order to save money

All-in-one studio package

Some showreel companies will do the whole thing for you, filming and editing scenes to create a professional-looking reel (and they may also incorporate any footage you already have). These studios range in quality, so you have to do your research, with one actor warning, 'higher prices doesn't always indicate better quality'.

Consider this option if:

- You don't have any material from professional productions
- You want to bulk out your existing footage and you don't have the skills and contacts to shoot scenes and edit them yourself

Shooting a monologue on your phone or laptop

This is an option if you want something basic as a reference for casting teams and agents; useful if you're new to the profession. The tips in Chapter 12 (Self-taping) will show you how to create something as professional as possible. The advice from editors and casting directors is to use your own accent (you can add further monologues in other accents you're confident in). Upload your monologue/s to any casting sites you're a member of.

Beyond the standard reel

Once you've created your main reel, a further possibility is a genre-reel, featuring footage of you working in a specific style (for example, comedy or period-drama), or as one editor explains, 'you can have a version that's specifically for the American market with your American scene/s at the front'. If you have enough credits in one area, a genre-reel allows you to tailor your marketing, with one top casting director saying they 'save me time'.

Another option is to create specific reels related to individual projects – a 'Scenes from ...' reel. A few actors I spoke to say this is useful if you've had a recurring role in a TV series or appeared in a number of scenes in a single episode, film or short film. A 'Scenes from ...' reel is particularly effective if the project is prestigious or it shows off a specific aspect of your casting.

What to include in a reel

Casting teams and agents say the impact of your reel/s largely depends on who's watching; each viewer makes their own assessment of an actor's ability and how relevant their casting-range is to the projects they work on. However, while the effectiveness of your showreel is partly out of your hands, there is still plenty of advice on how to increase your chances of impressing.

Finding the right editor/studio

If you're using an editor or studio to create your reel then it's important to check out their work before you buy; make sure it's the right quality and style for the level and/or area of the industry you're targeting. And always check the pricing and how the added extras stack up, including how much it costs to reedit or add footage to your reel later down the line.

Most actors I spoke to found an editor via recommendations, often from other actors. If you're represented, speak to your agent; they may suggest someone or, as was the case for one actor I spoke to, even offer to put a reel together themselves. For a wider range of studios and editors, look in the *Actors and Performers Yearbook* or simply type 'showreel editors' in Google.

Getting hold of clips

'Get clips in the highest quality possible,' a studio editor advises, adding 'have a dialogue about whether or not your editor can source material at good quality'. If not, then they recommend 'downloading on iTunes – it looks and sounds better'. Alternatively, actors I spoke to had found clips by (if represented) checking to see what their agent had, contacting production companies directly, going through any friends who are currently working on that show or (last resort) paying for a copy on disc. Once you've got your clips, make sure that before your session you've noted the timings of any scenes you want to use.

Keep it short

This is the shiny, golden rule when it comes to creating a showreel. Casting teams and agents I spoke to all say they're too busy to watch long reels, and they will extract the information they need by skimming through or watching just one or two scenes. One director explains that it also just comes down to practicalities: 'We have hundreds of applications on Spotlight alone for any show we're casting. If every actor has a showreel that's three minutes long ... well, you do the maths on that.'

If you're starting out, using several scenes you've shot yourself just to get a foot in the door, then an editor advises, 'you don't want to be going longer than 90 seconds really, two minutes at most'. Three minutes is usually given as the ideal maximum length for a reel that is made up of several professional scenes; at the upper limit another editor says, 'you could get away with five minutes if you really want to put a big range of stuff; just know that if you have ten minutes of fantastic stuff, nobody is going to watch that all the way through except your Mum.'

One final thing to consider is having a Twitter-friendly version of your reel. As an editor explains, getting your showreel under two minutes twenty seconds, or having a version of it at this length, 'means you can then upload directly. Twitter is a great place to have your reel early in your career; you can promote yourself with things like #showreelshareday.'

Types of scenes to include

According to the industry, your reel should show off your main casting type/s, your casting range, your impressive credits and, of course, your acting ability. Not every actor will have scenes that do all of these things at once but meeting one or more of these criteria with each scene is a useful aim.

Practise some quality control. The most basic criteria for including a scene is that it shows you acting well, and remember, anything that's shot badly will make you look amateurish, advertising you in all the wrong ways.

At their shortest, scenes can be a matter of seconds; at their longest, one editor I spoke to recommends '30–40 seconds', with a producer revealing, 'if you've got a three minute showreel and you've got three scenes in it, I'm probably only going to look at the first ten seconds of each'.

Scenes you're the lead of or a major part in work best, but if you don't have these, you or an editor can cut around other actors to make you appear more heavily involved. While it's advised you include at least one scene where you're featured talking, casting directors and agents say you can use scenes with little or no dialogue. Again, use your editing skills or rely on your editor to make the most of any dialogue you do have.

One director says, 'if you've been in anything good [your reel] is an opportunity to bang that point home'. Others agree, saying that very short scenes alongside a star actor or on a high-profile project are fine to put in if you have a line or two and can be seen properly. Almost everyone advised against including scenes filmed from plays or musicals, the only exception being if the footage is brilliantly shot (something like NT Live).

How old can your material be? As one editor I asked explains, 'if you're a younger actor you probably don't have to worry about this, if you're slightly older but haven't aged much you'll be able to get away with more, and obviously, if you haven't got newer stuff to use then you don't have much choice. Optimally scenes shouldn't be more than a few years old, but there is a balance between how cool something is and how old it is; if you had a scene with Tom Cruise from a decade ago, keep it in, because it's Tom Cruise. A good rule as you come to reedit your reel is to use the most recent and/or most high-profile scenes you have; and that will probably mean you lose the older stuff over time.'

If you're choosing scenes to film for your reel, then the advice from an experienced editor is: 'don't do incredibly famous scenes, scenes that are associated strongly with an actor'. They also point out that 'a lot of what we see on television now is much more real life, much more naturalistic, whereas a lot of the scripts sometimes people tend to bring in are very theatrical. You look at it and go, "I just don't believe what I'm seeing here."' Understanding your casting is key when selecting scenes: 'Agents say to us relevance is the most important thing: your reel shows off characters they are actually going to be able to sell! If you know the direction you want to push yourself in, you can tailor whatever scene or scenes you do to go, "These are my strong points."'

One editor highlights that music-laden montages at the beginning of a reel 'are the bugbear of every casting director'. Another agrees, saying, 'go with your strong acting content, get some solid scenes in there and don't try and montage up a student film to make it look like it's a Hollywood blockbuster'. Montages 'can still serve a purpose. If you've got lots of good moments that you couldn't put into a longer scene that you still feel you should really show, then perhaps have a little round-up at the end to go, "Here are my long-form scenes, and here are also some other projects I've done that are brief but don't really make scenes."' If you are considering a montage later in your reel then, as another editor warns, 'you'll need a studio or a certain amount of skill yourself ... don't even try it if you're not sure'.

Putting the scenes in order

A busy showreel studio head offers some guidelines on choosing your first scene. 'A showreel is a selling tool, so put your strongest foot forward. You might be proudest of a role where you played a mime, and it's the most artistic thing you've done and it's brilliantly shot, and you love it because you invested so much personal time in it ... but it's not the most sellable thing for you in terms of getting you on to television, or getting you into the agency's door.'

They outline that 'for a general purpose your first scene should look like you and sound like you – if it's for the UK market put a scene with your own accent on the front – reflecting how you're going to get yourself into the market most easily. Or it should be something that makes them go, "Wow, that's a big job, they're obviously good" ... so if you've been in a blockbuster and you happen to have a French accent in it, then fine, it's a blockbuster, stick it up front. You can even use a three-line moment from a film or show as a little pre-coda ... and then you're into a longer scene.' They explain, 'by starting with your most current or most high-profile or highest quality work, you can then round up your other pieces that perhaps aren't so high quality or relevant. Make a good impression with your first scene, and then people will make an allowance for what comes after that.'

Once you've decided on the first one or two scenes, they warn, 'you can very easily get bogged down in the minutiae thinking the order of the fourth and fifth clips is going to be the absolute game-changer for your showreel. But there is no hard and fast rule; you have to just see how all your different bits of footage interact with each other and try and find the best way through. It's about how does all of your footage work together as a package? ... and making that flow.'

Their final piece of advice is to not overcomplicate things: 'Coming back in to the same scene or project three times is a bugbear. Cutting the scene into four pieces doesn't make it easier to watch, or more dynamic; it just makes it look rubbish, and the casting director will go, "Well, I've seen this, why am I seeing it again?" If it's a good scene, let it be a good scene. If it's too long, cut it down.'

Title cards and scene labels

If you're creating a showreel yourself then, as one editor says, 'you don't need fancy titles'. Open the reel with your name on a black background. Finish with your agent's name and contact details, or your details if you're not represented (if you have a good website include the address). If you're including scenes from professional productions, quickly include the name of the project and the production company over the first few frames of each scene in the bottom left corner; or the name of each scene and the director. If all your scenes are home-made then the general advice is to leave off-scene labelling. For genre-reels and 'Scenes from …' reels be sure the title card clearly states what type of reel the viewer is about to watch: for example, 'John Brown, Comedy Reel'; 'Rosa Smith, TV Show X' or 'Rosa Smith, Scenes from TV Show X'.

Using your reel

If you're represented, send a version of your finished reel to your agent. Upload it on to your Spotlight page and other casting sites, IMDb Pro or sites like Vimeo. You can get your reel into other areas of online marketing, including Twitter if it's short enough.

If you're sending your reel out to casting teams about specific roles or genres of work, follow the advice of one actor/editor: 'Draw someone's attention to specific parts of the reel. If you've got that scene where you're a cockney and that's what you want them to see, mention how far into the reel the scene appears so they can go straight to it.' Or as another editor advises, if you have the skills, 'tailor your reel. If you get a call for a job which requires a French accent, get that fourth scene with a French accent and stick it up front.'

Think of a showreel as a work in progress, reflecting your changing selling points as your career develops. Whenever you can, update it with new material, and find the right time to upgrade or add supplementary reels to improve your package of marketing materials.

Smartening up your email

Always look professional!

Career coach

Interviewees offer a few simple tips on how to make sure any emails you send out to the industry look smart and advertise your selling points. The first thing to do, as one actor advises, is to make sure your address isn't 'something you're going to cringe at'. Casting teams and agents advise choosing something as close as possible to your professional acting name, using underscores, dots or initials if necessary.

Second, add a photo. Many actors choose a colour headshot, but you can use something more relaxed as long as it doesn't look unprofessional. Third, add signatures – the snippets of information that appear at the bottom of your email. You can include links to your representation, IMDb, website, showreel or Spotlight. This is normally fairly easy to set up: for example, in Gmail go to Settings; if you're using Mail through a Mac go to Preferences.

Fourth, learn to use links. These allow industry figures to view websites in one click, which makes viewing your Spotlight page or showreel, for example, much easier. Hyperlinks mean your recipient can click on a word (e.g. 'Please click here to view my showreel'). Again, these are fairly easy to get to grips with: on Gmail highlight the word, click on the little chain link ('Insert links') on the tools menu at the bottom of the email, and copy and paste in a web address; for Mail on Macs highlight the word, go to Edit and then Add Link.

Finally, figure out how to include a headshot. For Mail on Macs, click attach, choose your photo and select 'Small' size, and your headshot should appear in the main body of your email. With other servers it may be copy-or-paste or insert; google yours to find out how.

For free resources to help you make the most of the expert advice in this chapter, visit www.actorscareerbible.com/freestuff

PART TWO
FINDING WORK

4
CASTING SITES

This chapter covers advice on sites like Mandy.com, Spotlight and the Equity Job Information Service; any online service that helps you apply for work yourself.

Use the advice in this chapter to work on:

- Choosing casting sites that suit your career stage and budget
- Using the sites effectively

Are casting sites worth it for you?

Worth it? Depends on your place in the industry. If you're new to the game you are trying to establish any foothold you can.

Actor, seven years in the profession

Advice suggests that looking for work through casting sites will benefit most actors at early career stages. If you're new to the profession, a proactive performer calls the sites 'a great starting point', with another explaining some of the auditions available offer 'an easier learning environment, building up your comfort with going to meetings and preparing scripts'. In fact, for several actors I spoke to, casting sites led to important firsts: 'My first audition'; 'My first paid gig'; 'My first useful industry relationship'; 'My first showreel'; 'My first agent'.

If you're slightly further into your career, you can still benefit. Unrepresented actors interviewed use the sites to find jobs and – by building showreel material and looking for chances to showcase themselves on stage – as a means to attract agents. Many of the represented actors interviewed use casting sites to supplement the opportunities they are getting from their agent or as part of a plan to look for new representation.

The only group not using casting sites for finding work were represented actors consistently looking for paid jobs above a certain level, with one telling me, 'you'll know when you've reached the point when they are no longer a useful option'. Casting teams working on higher-level projects say they rarely open castings out, with a busy London theatre producer explaining, 'only if it's something very niche, a role with very specific physical characteristics like loads of tattoos or they're particularly tall or short. If not, then most of the people who we'll be realistically considering will be submitted through agents.'

Choosing the right sites

(Our site) is for the proactive actor who goes looking for opportunities rather than waiting for the opportunity to come to them.
                                                    Staff at a popular casting site

There are plenty of casting sites to choose from. The bigger ones, such as Mandy.com, allow you to apply for jobs directly and offer lots of added extras. Others post auditions and contact details, which you can then use to apply for work yourself either via email or an agent if represented. While most list a range of auditions, some sites specialize in screen or stage projects.

Actors recommend you be selective, picking out the best site/s for your particular career stage and budget. Being choosy will also keep your workload manageable, with one recent graduate explaining, 'you can get enough off one or two sites … (otherwise) it can be too complicated to keep track'. There are three steps here. First, use the advice in this section to work out your priorities. Second, based on those priorities, ask around among friends and check online testimonials; a regular casting site user says, 'you'll quickly learn which ones are time-wasters and which are worth investing in'. Finally, as another casting site veteran advises, 'experiment with a range'. Many sites offer a free trial period, low-cost package or a cancellable monthly fee so you can usually give them a good go before committing fully.

Prioritizing for your career stage and budget

If you don't yet have many professional credits or training, you can still make use of casting sites. One actor advises first testing restricted sites by being a little creative with your credits: 'Put down any shows or showcases you've done from courses and short films as well.' If you still don't get accepted, then move on to sites 'where you don't need any experience or you need to have a single credit to join, applying for jobs that will earn you access to other more restricted sites'. A good starting place is a site like the Stage Castings.

If you've reached the point where you want regular access to the best auditions casting sites offer, the advice is you'll need to sign up for full membership on at least one of the more restricted sites, with a theatre producer-director saying, 'most of the people I know towards the lower end of the industry that are serious about pushing on will either be on Spotlight[1] or Mandy.com or both'.

For most actors, costs are a big decision factor here, with one explaining, 'I wouldn't be able to join more than one paid site outside of Spotlight.' To get the most out of your budget, the advice is to take advantage of trial periods, look out for the discounts sometimes offered by organizations such as the Actors' Guild and check out new sites offering introductory packages. If you're on a really tight budget, sites that focus on one area can still be a good option. For example, actors told me they used sites like Shooting People to build material for their showreels without having to splash out heavily, and a site like Dramanic was recommended if your focus is on theatre projects.

---

[1]Spotlight is a slightly special case. If you're represented, you can't use Spotlight to apply for jobs directly yourself; however, your agent will almost certainly expect you to be on the site so that they can submit you for work. You will still be able to see lists of casting breakdowns and suggest things to your agent, and one actor also adds, 'your agent can change a setting that allows you to nudge them if you see a role you think you might be a good fit for.' Be aware that not every agent will be keen on this!

Using casting sites

Don't get obsessed!

Actor, two years using casting sites

Upload voice clips, showreels and photos to your casting site profiles. Your main photo should show off your main casting type (if unsure, the advice is to pick something fairly neutral that's close to the 'everyday' you). Include two to three other headshots to reflect the rest of your range (you can also include a black-and-white version of your main shot). Only use production shots from plays and screen if your headshots don't cover an important area of your casting.

Casting directors' advice is to only include accents and skills you can have audition-ready if called for a meeting. If you've not trained formally, a leading TV casting director suggests including top coaches you've worked with extensively and any summer schools or training courses you've been on.

The general advice for actors with only a handful of credits is to include everything you can. This approach has the obvious advantage of making you look busy, and as one casting director told me, 'we're always interested to see if you've worked with someone we know of or perhaps admire'. Include your credits while training, especially if they indicate your casting, you had a big/well-known part, you appeared in an interesting play or worked with a professional director. Workshops, readings, short films etc. can fill out your CV and give even more clues to your casting. Leave out Supporting Artist (extra) work and amateur credits.

Profile pages normally have a space for your biography. For most sites, the advice is to use the third person, summing up your main credits and selling points in a few sentences. On Spotlight, the equivalent is the 'Currently appearing' section. Actors I spoke to use this for three main things: to indicate they are in demand, to advertise upcoming performances or to alert the industry to their upcoming availability. While one actor I spoke to uses the 'Currently Appearing' section on Spotlight as a mini-biography, the general advice is to keep things punchy; for example, 'Currently appearing in *Romeo and Juliet* directed by X at Theatre X, till 29th April'. Include what stage you're at with the production (e.g. 'Will begin rehearsals for/am currently rehearsing/am appearing/featuring in/have recently finished ...'). If relevant, you can also add in the size of the role (e.g. lead or co-lead for theatre, as well as supporting, series regular, semi-regular or guest for TV), the names of prominent actors involved ('Appearing alongside ...'), quotes from any reviews, information about any nominations or awards you or the project has received, a link to the production's website or a link to clips of the film/TV show that you are hosting on a site like Vimeo. You could also include a link to catch-up sites like BBC iPlayer (with the time-code of your first appearance or main scenes if you have a smaller part). If you're currently unemployed, you can create the impression that you've been busy by using a phrase like 'Recently appeared in ...' or 'Recently finished ...' for a few weeks after a job. However, casting directors say it is absolutely ok to leave this section blank; all this shows is that you're currently available for auditions and work.

Finding castings to apply for

According to one actor, 'if you think a casting is interesting and that you might fit it and you can make the dates and it sounds like the people have half a brain, then apply'. Fairly simple! As another actor outlines, 'when you start, drop your standards; look at everything, paid and unpaid. Once you get a bit under your belt, you can be stricter about what you want to do and not do, and what you end up applying for.'

If you're struggling to motivate yourself, then work towards a goal; for example, applying for a set number of jobs a day, week or month. On the other hand, if casting sites are not your main priority then, as one actor warns, 'it's easy to apply for lots of jobs and spread yourself too thin. And it's costly, both financially and time-wise preparing and getting to auditions in God-knows where.' To combat this, another actor told me they only use the sites 'when I'm not getting anything external (through their agent or industry connections)'.

Putting together effective submissions

A director outlines how they receive applications through sites like Spotlight and Mandy.com: 'We initially see a page with lots of people's headshots and half a tweets worth of text. The first step for us is asking who are the "Yes"s, "No"s and "Maybe"s.'

To improve your chances, first of all, 'don't be in the group of people that get cut just from their headshot alone', they warn. If you haven't already got a range of good quality photos, go to Chapter 2 for advice. Then, whenever you can, pick a headshot that suits the particular casting. As our director explains, this is fairly simple: 'If you've got three headshots and you're going up for the gangster role then pick you're most gangster-looking headshot.' Sorted!

Second, be concise when filling in comment boxes, cover letters or additional information sections. Our director-interviewee says during their initial Yes/No/Maybe sweeps, 'we only see the first few lines of what you've written. If you put, "Dear Mr Director, thank you very much for your time ..." that's all I can see, and if I want to read anymore then I've got to click on it.' Their advice, therefore, is to start with 'two-three bullet points; something that's makes you right for that part'. Others echoed this, with one experienced casting director saying, 'it helps to make a small comment but not a whole breakdown of why you're right for the part and all that ... people write a whole screen's worth. I just skip through it.'

Below are examples suggested by casting teams and experienced actors (if you're worried about this approach, then you can include more detail below your bullet points so they see it if they click on your submission). As one casting director explains, highlight your strengths: 'Make a comment that ticks a box on the character breakdown. If I'm casting for a Brazilian part then it helps if you put you're a native of that place, or that you're from Argentina or somewhere nearby.'

Examples

For a part at a fringe theatre in Manchester:

Manchester resident.

Recently performed at the National Theatre with director X

For a small part as a midlands car mechanic:

LAMDA-trained. Worked as a car mechanic for 5 years. Midlands.

Success – and patience! – with casting sites

As with every method of finding acting work, results from casting sites may not be immediate; as one actor admits, 'you have to sift through a lot of shit and go to a lot of auditions to find things that are good and worth your time'. Casting site users say it helps to accept and expect 'No's and non-responses, and put your attention solely towards regularly sending quality submissions. As one actor explains, after applying, 'I try to completely forget about it, and if I get a response, then I'm like "Oh wow, great."' Remember that one successful submission is worth months of repeated applying, and that interviewees have found jobs and fruitful industry relationships by persisting with casting sites.

For free resources to help you make the most of the expert advice in this chapter, visit www.actorscareerbible.com/freestuff

5
DIRECT CONTACT

This chapter covers advice on sending emails (and the odd letter) to people in the industry. Direct contact is useful for many aspects of your career, including applying for auditions and inviting casting teams to see your work.

Use the advice in this chapter to work on:

- Understanding the principles behind effective direct contact
- Applying for jobs
- Inviting industry to see your work
- Making the most of other opportunities for emailing

Using direct contact effectively

Be more like a laser than a shot-gun.

Successful screen actor

Interviewees for this guide offer several key guidelines for creating effective direct contact. Start by smartening up your email, making sure you have a professional-sounding address, adding a photo and signature, and learning how to use links and send headshots (all of this is covered in Chapter 3).

Avoid mass mail-outs. As one career coach underlines, 'copy and paste is obvious to (casting teams) and a massive No-No'. Instead, tailor your emails to your recipients: 'Research will give you meaningful content, and whether they bring you in or not, they will always remember that person.' *Always* do your research when contacting someone new: given the actors they normally cast, are they likely to be interested in your current selling points? You can research casting teams using the sources listed on page 16.

Perhaps most importantly, make sure you always have a specific reason for getting in touch. One casting director emphasizes, 'I don't want just a random email. Unless it's about a show or it's something relevant to what I'm casting, I don't really look at them,' while another says, 'don't send "Wondering if there is anything happening?" or "Please think of me for anything that is suitable" … because, well, yeah, that is what I do.'

Beyond those more practical tips, there is lots of advice on motivating yourself to email off. Casting teams are generally positive about actors approaching them. 'We know everyone wants to get seen,' says one casting director, with another explaining, 'The industry needs a turnover of actors, and finding new interesting people is what we enjoy.' An experienced producer meanwhile encourages actors, saying, 'it's easier than ever to get email addresses and find out exactly how people like to be contacted. Listen to a podcast and you get great casting agents telling you, "Don't send me a big letter, send me a couple of lines, your CV and a link to your stuff."'

Patience is key. A British actor working in America revealed that at the start of their career the hit rate was low ('out of every 80 or 100 emails I would get one or two replies'). But they went on to explain that '1% reward can be a career-changer. If you get in with one casting director that could be two jobs with them, and that will bring you to the attention of all the people you wrote to previously.' Another successful actor echoes this, saying, 'if they feel you're castable in a certain area then, sometimes months or years later people get brought in. Or people you wrote to years ago may by chance see you perform and take more notice of you and be more likely to get you in.'

Not getting a reply therefore doesn't mean you haven't made an impression. 'I might not come to see your show,' says one casting director, 'but I've had the contact, the name's stuck a bit and I'm aware of what you're doing.' They add, 'it's impossible to reply to everyone, it really is, and I will probably only reply to people I know or have requested information from'.

Your strategy should be, as an experienced performer explains, to see 'contact as an ongoing process', focusing largely on your most realistic targets given your current strengths to increase the likelihood of getting a response. Write without expectation of reply, trust your emails will be read and that you'll be kept in mind when the time's right. Couple direct contact with other forms of marketing, and you'll give yourself a good chance of eventually getting on casting teams' radars.

General advice on putting together emails

'Get to the point in your emails,' says one casting director bluntly. The only exception to the 'keep it brief' rule is if you're trying to convey your passion for a particular project, in which case you may want to go into more length. This is also one of the few times actors suggest considering posting rather than emailing.

Finding the right tone can be tricky if you're writing to someone new. 'We are either fearful and not confident enough or we are over-confident and over-familiar,' a career coach explains, 'so you end up either blowing smoke or you come across as if you've just left drama school and think you own the world.' They, like many, advise you aim for a balance between ease and being clear, polite and professional.

Interviewees suggest various common elements you can pick and choose to include in your emails (throughout the rest of the chapter there are more specific tips on what to include, when):

- 'Dear [their first name]', as opposed to 'Dear Sir/Madam' or anything else in general. Choose 'Dear X' if you've not had much previous contact; 'Hi X' if you're more familiar or replying

- An introductory greeting along the lines of 'Hope you're well' or 'How are you?'

- Something positive about your current situation: for example, you are currently graduating, you are a recent graduate, you've been cast in a show or you are coming to the end of a job. If you can, link this to their work in some way; for example, mention the name of an actor you're working alongside that they've previously cast

- A reminder of any previous relationship you have with them. A career coach suggests various ways to do this: 'Great seeing you last time at/for …'; 'Last time we spoke you were just about to start X. I saw it and thought …'; 'Last time I saw you at X I was just about to go and do Y. It went really well … here's a clip'

- The name of anyone who's prompted you to make contact. As an experienced casting director explains, 'when it's a friend of a friend, you pay a bit more attention'

- Compliments on their previous work. The advice from a career coach here is 'keep it really brief, genuine and very specific. Telling them you loved their most famous show or listing off most of the projects on their CV doesn't necessarily make that good an impression'

- The reason you're emailing; for example, details of the project you're applying for or the show you're inviting them to

- Anything that makes you right for their casting; for example, aspects of your look or your previous credits

- An invite to see your work that supports another reason for emailing them. If you're applying for a casting, for example, add an invite to see you perform

- A link to a showreel if you have one: for example, 'My showreel is here'

- A link to a CV: for example, 'My CV is here'

- A photo in the main body of your email (see page 45 if you're unsure how to do this)

- An informal but professional-enough sign-off: for example, 'Many thanks' or 'Best wishes'

Before sending a finished email, several interviewees recommend sending a test version to yourself, checking the formatting and links. Once your email is finally gone, contact anyone who has recommended you or said you could drop their name; let them know you've sent something, and thank them. Make a note of what you've sent to who, when and any replies (see page 18 for more). If you're represented, you can also update your agent on who you've been contacting.

Replies and following up

Briefly acknowledge any replies you receive, positive or negative. However, following up – checking your emails have been received or asking for a response – is generally advised against, with a casting directing saying, 'if someone's not replied then just leave it'. Their advice in fact – along with many others – is to leave a decent gap before getting back in touch: 'It can get annoying if you get so many emails from the same person. That's when you go, "Oh no, not again." ' Suggestions vary on the right gap to leave, but perhaps the best advice comes from another casting director: 'Use "I've got something new to show you" as the rule; not "I haven't sent something for 6 months." '

Using direct contact to apply for jobs

We don't have to know you (for you to contact us). There might be something about you that's interesting in your look or your CV.

TV casting director

You can use direct contact to apply for job opportunities you come across – an alternative if you can't apply through an agent, or as a casting director suggests, 'if you've missed the deadline on Spotlight (or any other casting site)'. If you're represented, occasionally sending a supplementary email yourself may help your chances; consult your agent on this.

Put some thought into what you apply for, making sure you're close to the casting types, and – unless the skills, accents or looks required are niche – you have some relevant experience or quality training. Any previous relationship or link you have with the casting team will also help your case.

If you decide the opportunity is realistically worth applying for, do your research: look for details about the casting team and their previous work, the role and anything in particular they're looking for, contact details, any information on how they prefer to be contacted and any links between you.

Your research will help you create a tailored email that advertises your selling points. The basic elements to include in an audition-application email are:

- Dear/Hi [their first name]
- An introductory greeting
- If relevant, a reminder of any previous relationship you have to them, a recommendation or a more tenuous link
- Something positive about your current situation
- Any very brief and genuine compliments on their previous work
- The reason you're emailing: for example, 'I would love to be considered for X.' Where possible, name the role or roles you think you are right for
- Why you're right for the role: for example, your casting types, special skills, previous experience, connections to the project or passion for a particular aspect of the project. Present these as matter-of-factly as you can: for example, 'I've played ice-hockey for England,' 'I'm 6 ft 7,' 'I recently played Ophelia on tour,' 'As a native of Southern Ireland, I could really relate to . . .'
- An invitation to see your work if you have something relevant coming up
- A link to a showreel if you have one
- A link to a CV
- A sign-off
- A photo

If you're unsure about any of these, there's further advice on pages 59–60. Don't crowbar any of these elements in if it feels like a stretch. Remember, keeping things brief, genuine and specific will help your cause.

Unless you have better information, apply as soon as you hear about a casting. If you're coupling your application with an invite to a performance, ideally give your recipient at least a fortnight's notice (as mentioned on page 64, if you're giving a decent amount of notice, you can send a reminder in the days before your performance begins).

For your subject heading use the name of the project and role (e.g. 'Tybalt – Romeo and Juliet casting'). If you can, include anything else that might catch their eye: for example, if you have a previous relationship, include your name and perhaps a related project; or if you've been recommended, include the name (e.g. 'Via . . .').

Using direct contact to invite casting teams to your upcoming performances

We work a full week, go to the theatre in the evening and have families and the rest of our lives going on. So it is difficult to get us to come to your show unless it is something we have a reason to see: a play that we're interested in, actors we're interested in, a venue that is easy to get to, or an agent that is involved that we like working with.
Experienced casting director

As the quote above suggests, you have to be realistic about the number of industry people who'll take up your invites, with one experienced actor saying grimly, 'don't expect many or even any to come'. Don't be put-off, however, especially if you're focusing on people you already have some sort of relationship with. And remember that you'll still benefit by signalling to casting teams that you're working. If you're represented, discuss invites with your agent first; they may be able to bring along someone on your list without you having to write off.

You can be fairly informal if you're inviting industry figures you already have a strong previous relationship with. One successful actor suggests something along the lines of '… Just to let you know, I'm doing a play. If you are around it would be great if you could come and see it; I think it's going to be good. Hope you're well . . .'

For casting teams you're less familiar with, you'll need to put a bit more thought in. Focus on those operating around your career level and whose work relates in some way to your project (one experienced TV casting director explains, 'I'm probably not going to go and see you in *Twelfth Night*'). If you're performing outside the capital, don't be afraid to invite London-based people, but give plenty of notice. 'I can't travel across the country at short notice,' the same casting director says. 'I'm based in London, so don't invite me to a lunchtime show in Liverpool cos I'm not going to go.' If you're unsure about who to target, go to Chapter 2 for advice.

Research before making contact. You're looking for accurate contact details, anything on how they prefer to be contacted and any links between the two of you. Again, there's further advice in Chapter 2.

Casting directors recommend giving at least two weeks' notice for your performances. If you want to be a bit more strategic here, then some actors suggest making contact at an earlier point (when you get the role or start rehearsals, for example) and then, even if you've not received a reply, sending a reminder email a week or so before the performance.

How many people can you invite to a show or screening? 'The big difference between writing to agents and casting directors,' a career coach explains, 'is the number you will write to. Rather than 10 or so agents, it could be 50 casting directors. Write them in bulks of five to ten. "These are the first 10 casting directors I really want to come" … start with them. This gives you the chance to personalize them – you can do that in a group of 10 emails – rather than scattershot, which tends not to work.'

The basic elements to include in an invite email are:

- Dear [their first name] ('Hi …' if you already have some sort of relationship)
- An introductory greeting
- If relevant, a reminder of any previous relationship you have to them, a recommendation or a more tenuous link
- Something positive about your current situation
- Any very brief and very genuine compliments on their previous work
- The reason you're emailing, that is, the details of your invite
- Why you're right for their type of work: for example, your casting types, special skills, previous experience, connections to or passion for the work they do
- A link to a showreel if you have one
- A link to a CV

- A sign-off
- A photo

If you're unsure about any of these, there's further advice on pages 59–60. Again, don't force in any elements you don't need, especially if you're confident your recipient will be interested in your show; simply send a polite email with the details of your invite.

The advice here applies for inviting casting directors or other industry figures. For plays, include the name of the show, the part, the venue, the dates and times, and an offer to sort tickets. If you can, highlight any relevant selling points that aren't obvious (e.g. 'It's a new comedy' or 'I'm appearing alongside Well Known Actor X'), if the show is short ('It's an hour long') and if it's convenient to get to if not a well-known venue ('... just outside Central London').

For TV, include the name of the show, the part, when it is on and what channel. If it's one or two scenes, indicate how far in you appear: 'My first appearance/my main scene is ten minutes in.' If your appearance is going to be on a catch-up service, send a link and the time at which your scene/s appear. If it's a film you're in, let them know where and when they can see it.

If you're emailing a casting director you know has already seen you perform, then remind them and adapt the previous advice accordingly: for example, 'Thank you for coming to see/I understand you recently saw *Romeo and Juliet* ...'; 'X (their client) told me you'd been in to see *Romeo and Juliet* . . ..'

For your subject heading, include the name of the show or screening. Casting directors say you can also include the name of anyone who's recommended you (e.g. 'Recommended by X'). You could also choose to include your name and any major strengths that are relevant to their casting.

Further uses for direct contact

Our industry is just memory ... produce memory!

Career coach

Interviewees suggest plenty of other ways you can use direct contact, each of which is listed over the following pages. Despite the number of suggestions, be wary of inundating casting teams; leave decent gaps each time you get in contact, always making sure you have a really good reason.

Updates and nudges for casting teams you already know

Send out little 'information-bites', as one actor calls them, to people you haven't been in touch with for a while, updating them with your latest news. Use the subject heading: 'Quick Update: Your name/Name of a relevant production'.

Suggested opportunities:

- Update casting teams about your last job, taking advantage of the just-been-in-work grace period: 'I was recently working at . . . ' or 'I was recently working with . . . .' This is especially useful if your last job is relatable in some way to the person you are writing to; for example, you recently did a laugh-out-loud play and are writing to a casting director specializing in comedy. If it's a screen performance, edit and send out some clips, with an email along the lines of, 'If you didn't catch it last night/week/month here are my scenes'

- If you're coming to the end of a job, email potential employers to let them know (1) that you've been working and had a wonderful time and (2) you are now/will very soon be available to audition

- Advertise new marketing materials: 'Here are my new headshots/ my latest showreel'

- Update people if your circumstances change. For example, email previous employers about your brand new agent

Introduce yourself to new casting teams

If you have a showreel you're happy with, use this as a means to introduce your work to new casting teams. Find realistic targets and then, as one experienced performer advises, 'write to them all, and note when you have done it. Then wait till you have something new to say or show them and remind them of when you first wrote.' Another way to introduce yourself to new casting teams is to make the most of any links you have with them. For example, one performer touring their home town emailed the casting department of the local theatre: 'I said, "I'm from the area, I'm appearing in a show, do you fancy meeting up?" They said, "Yes!" '

Follow-up on what you've seen and loved

Contact the director, producer or casting director of productions you've enjoyed and let them know what you thought (if you have a genuine passion and knowledge for someone's work then a letter can be effective). One bold actor told me, 'I email asking the director if I can treat them for a coffee', an approach that can work if you have a link to them in some way or credits they might be interested in.

Write to get involved

There are many organizations that run classes, workshops and talks where you can meet industry people while developing your acting or marketing skills; contact them to see if you can get involved. And if you're on a job, don't wait to be asked to readings and workshops; email the relevant department showing your interest. Actors say you can take advantage of other facilities and opportunities at theatres while you're working; for example, check with literary departments to get hold of new plays that are coming up or, if you have your own work or writing you want to rehearse or present, ask if there is a space you can use.

And once you've got involved … write off

If you've done a workshop, taken a course or been to a seminar, not only can you follow-up with the people you've met, but also use your latest experience as a basis for writing to new companies and employers: 'I've just finished workshopping with. . ..'

'Nice to meet/see you's

As you go about your daily life as performer, you'll bump into people in the industry, whether it be on a project, at a networking event, an industry-related party or even just seeing a show. Actors suggest sending a quick 'Nice-to-meet/see-you' follow-up email and use the same thread for future correspondence.

Reopen old doors

Actors say a quick email can help you reconnect with people you've lost touch with: an ex-mentor, a director you worked with at drama school or a friend from the first play you did. Say hello, find out what they're up to and you may rebuild a useful old connection.

Say 'thank you' … and avoid burning bridges

Maintaining good relations can be as simple as sending a quick email; a 'Thank you' for someone who's helped you out is easy, kind and leaves a good impression. Do this without an agenda ('It has to be genuine!' says one actor, 'not to say anything other than that you're grateful') and you can't go far wrong.

Suggested opportunities:

- To a casting director if you've just been cast or are coming to the end of an enjoyable project. One actor suggests doing this towards Christmas: 'I contacted a casting director to thank them for turning my year around … they got me back in!' Their advice is that this is an instance where you don't necessarily have to go with an email: 'I try sending something worth keeping; an arty postcard, something related to the project'

- A casting director sends you a 'No' for whatever reason; send a quick email to thank them for getting back to you

- Someone in the industry has been in to see your show

- Someone has given you good advice you've acted on

- A friend or contact has helped you on a personal project

For free resources to help you make the most of the expert advice in this chapter, visit www.actorscareerbible.com/freestuff

6
FINDING THE RIGHT AGENT

For a few of the represented actors interviewed for this guide, finding the right agent was a simple process; they were approached at drama school, spotted performing or recommended by someone with influence. The majority, however, approached agents themselves. This chapter will take you through each stage of that process, giving you the best chance of finding the right agent for you.

Use the advice in this chapter to work on:

- Getting everything in place before making approaches
- Creating an effective submission
- Navigating agent meetings
- Handling offers
- Dealing with a 'No' at any point

Preparing to approach agents

The agent-game is fickle.

Experienced TV and theatre actor

Before you start sending off emails, interviewees suggest five preparatory steps. Use these to decide if it's the best time to make an approach and to increase your chances if you do choose to submit.

Find an opportunity to showcase your work

Agents say that in 99.9 per cent of cases they want to see an actor in action before they consider representing them. Interviewees suggest several showcasing options:

- A performance on stage: a play, an industry showcase or, if you're a final year actor, your course shows and showcases
- A performance on TV; as it airs and/or clips afterwards
- A screening of a film (feature-length and short) and/or clips afterwards
- A showreel

Ideally, there will be something obviously attractive about your show-casing opportunity. According to agents, this could be: the prestige of the venue, production company or drama course; the calibre of people you are working with; the size, complexity or attention-grabbing nature of the part/s; a link to the agent (for example, their client is involved in the production); or even the fact that you're not asking them to travel miles away from their office. However, if you have confidence in your performance, the advice is to be bold! Recent graduates interviewed emphasize that if you're a final year student, you don't necessarily need to be playing a lead role to get interest. And experienced actors say that if having looked at your headshot and/or CV an agent is interested, they may well consider travelling to see you in fringe theatre, festivals and screenings of short films.

Give agents a minimum of two to three weeks' notice when inviting them to see you perform; longer (advice suggests a maximum of six) if you're asking an agent to travel a long way, or you don't have many performance dates. In these cases, agents advise you also send a brief reminder either a few days before your showcase opportunity or along with snippets from any good reviews you get.

If you don't have an upcoming showcasing opportunity, then one option suggested by a career coach is industry showcases; 'sign up for several!' they urge. There are specialist showcases you can audition for all over the UK (e.g. Triforce), and some training organizations and classes also offer opportunities (e.g. The Actors Class). Another option is to focus your time on building up material for a showreel, getting it to a standard you're happy with (see Chapter 3 for more advice). A third possibility is to create your own work. Interviewees had shot and screened short films, while one actor interviewed produced an existing play at a small London venue and as a result signed with a leading agent. Their advice is to invite 'friends, and friends of friends, and if you can, ask them to bring their agents; the agents will then feel much more obliged to come'.

Alternatively, you can simply wait. Take some time to 'get yourself in as good a place as possible', advises an actor who'd hopped up the agent ladder: focus on your relationship with your current agent if you're represented, any other ways of finding work and being as ready as possible for auditions. At the same time, research a list of agents to submit to for when a showcasing opportunity does come up.

Sort your marketing materials

'You have one chance to impress!', an experienced actor highlights, so it's important to get your photos, CVs and showreel in the best shape possible before you apply. If you have the time and money, and you think there's room for improvement, go to Chapter 3 for advice.

Draw up a shortlist

Finding the *right* agent, a leading career coach explains, is about 'working out what you want *realistically* … and then looking for the person who is going to do that for you'. Rather than blanket-apply, take this targeted approach. You'll find the best fits for you, save the effort of sending out dozens and dozens of emails and, crucially, give yourself time to tailor your submissions (a top agent advises, 'don't be general – "I'm an actor wanting to get a new agent, I thought you'd be great". If you want a reply, target an agent and give a good reason why').

The first step to a targeted approach is to think about the working relationship you're after. For example, is it vital you have an agent who's happy to let you self-market? How personal/hands-off do you want the relationship to be? Is there anything about your particular circumstances that's important (e.g. one interviewee needed an agent who would be happy with them carrying on a blossoming music career)?

Second, ask yourself what's a realistic level of agent to target, given your previous experience? While all sorts of agents have successful actors on their books, interviewees often referred to a very general hierarchy, with one experienced actor describing 'a casting information flow that starts at the top and slows as it goes down', and another saying young actors 'need to know (which agents) are at the top, who's in the middle and who's in the bottom'. You can begin to get a sense of this by browsing agency websites comparing the level of clients' credits and by asking for opinions from people you trust in the industry. Once you have an idea, begin assessing where you might fit in. If you're a final year drama student or a very recent graduate your possibilities are fairly open; look at the range of agents that have signed actors from yours or similar courses. If you're slightly further in to your career, look for the type and level of work various agents' clients are doing, and compare how your credits or training stack up.

Thinking about the right working relationship and level will give you a 'profile' of agent to focus on (and probably some names that fit that profile). The next stage is look for more agents: they will either be definite 'No's, realistic fits, slightly more ambitious targets, or stand-by options.

To do this, go through listing guides like the *Actors and Performers Yearbook*, keep searching through agencies online and ask others for recommendations, letting people know the profile you're looking for. If you're a final year student, talk to staff, mentors and among your year group (one recent grad says, 'if a classmate signs with an agent before you do, use this as an opportunity to find out more about the agent and the business, without being a bore or stepping on your mate's toes'). Check with your school's box office to find out who's coming to see your shows and showcases (and have been in previous years). And keep looking up previous graduates and those from similar schools. If you're already in the profession, one actor says, 'gently let people you trust with influence know that you are looking for a new agent'. The 'trust' bit is important if you're represented; you don't want anything getting back to your current agent. Beyond seeking recommendations, consider any agents you have some sort of link to: for example, those that have considered you previously, have been to see your work, or have a client you know personally at the agency. If you're on an acting job or have one coming up, look at agents representing other cast-members around your career stage.

You may end up with quite a long list, in which case a career coach and successful actor suggests creating 'tiers' of six to eight submissions that you then work on in one go, 'so that you can properly focus on them'. They explain that with each tier 'you might focus on eight of your favourites first. Or you could mix it: one of your more ambitious choices, a few of your most realistic options and a couple of backups. Then once you've sent off your first tier move on to another 6 or so.'

Create a basic pitch

Another key preparatory step is to consider how you're going to sell yourself to prospective agents. At this stage you're simply coming up with ideas; the advice in the next sections will show you how to put these in to your emails and meetings.

Your 'pitch' will be made up of two elements. First, think about your selling points (if you're unsure, see Chapter 1). You can list your general strengths, but you'll increase your chances if you look through the eyes of the agents you're targeting; what will they find impressive or interesting, given the type of work their clients do?

The second part of your pitch is your reason/s for searching for new representation. If you're already in the profession, it's important to avoid being negative about your career or criticizing a current agent. As one leading agent explains, that's 'the worst because the agent you're approaching is going to think, "This person is a fucking nightmare" '. Instead, they say 'find positive reasons to join your prospective one. Turn any negative aspects of what has happened so far in your career into an aim for the future'. A career coach expands on this, explaining 'when you're making a request for representation, you are in fact making an offering: "I've got this far, but I need your help to take the next step." Don't ask them for something, offer them something!'

Actors gave plenty of examples of situations you can turn into an 'offer' for a new agent:

- You have a good set of previous credits. You're now looking for someone who can help you build on them, to take you to the next level

- You've worked in one particular style (e.g. comedy). You now want to move into a different genre

- You want help making the transition from small TV parts to theatre, or from the theatre parts you've been doing to TV opportunities

- You have lots of experience in one casting bracket, and now want help expanding your range

- You want to move on to a new age range of parts: for example, go from playing girls and teenagers to young women

- You have (are on or have recently finished) an exciting new job, and you want someone to help you capitalize on that

- You've just finished a long, successful job and want someone to help you make the transition back into the industry

- You've built up some good credits while based in another part of the country or the world but are now moving elsewhere and looking for an agent who can find work for you from there

- You've had a successful career in another profession and want help launching yourself into the acting industry

Finding the right way to make your approach

The final step before typing up your submissions is to find some sort of connection, however tenuous, with the agents you're approaching. As one career coach says, 'never go in without a link. You can try without, but it's probably going in the bin. Get a recommendation, find a connection or make one.'

'A personal recommendation massively helps,' says an experienced agent, and there are several options here. 'By far the best way', explains one actor, 'is through a casting director'. For this to work, you'll need to share a personal or close working relationship (i.e. you've been called in or cast by them several times). Contact the casting director explaining your reason/s for moving, your main selling points and the profile of agent you are looking for (with some of your own suggestions if you have them). Ask for advice: is this the right time to move and if so, can they suggest people to approach? Hopefully, they'll contact people on your behalf or give you permission to say they recommend you.

Actors interviewed did something similar with directors, producers, writers, well-connected teachers and coaches, and American managers and agents. Another option is a recommendation via a client at the agency you're targeting. The advice here is either gently bring up the topic to fish for some help or, if you're going to ask directly, do it sensitively, without putting pressure on the person to say 'Yes'. If a friend or contact does agree to help, then they can send an email on your behalf, message their agent asking them to look out for your upcoming email or allow you to mention their name in your email.

Another approach strategy is to use any offers and interest you've had from other agents. This can work as a seal of approval, and agents can become competitive! As one successful recent graduate outlines, 'if you're lucky to have a meeting with a top agent, immediately contact similar and smaller ones after – no matter how your meeting went – to say you're really keen to come in and talk about representation'.

If you can't use the strategies already mentioned, there are still ways to establish a link. If you've approached a particular agent before and received positive signals then that can be enough. The same goes if you know an agent has seen your previous work, or you have met them for some other reason; simply refer to it in your email.

In fact, interviewees say that any sort of vague connection is useful; for example, mentioning one of the agency's clients you have worked with, or even, as one career coach says, 'simply that you like [the agent's] work and what they have done throughout their career'. An experienced and successful actor suggests something similar: 'Look at their client's careers that you'd like to mirror. Then your angle is "My name is X; you represent Y, whose career resembles my own the closest . . ."'

Finally, if you're feeling especially tentative, an actor suggests, 'ask if you can just get an advice meeting'. Another explains that this 'approach creates less pressure', with another performer adding it can be easier to get a foot in the door, 'even if you end up getting referred to an assistant'. This option is also worth considering if you've had a recent change in circumstances: for example, you've had to leave your previous agent or, as in the case of one actor I spoke to, you've suddenly got a career-changing job. They explain they successfully changed agents by 'putting things in a slightly ambiguous way: "I'd be very grateful for any advice if you have the time"'. You could even consider not asking for anything at all. One or two actors told me they'd bumped into agents they were interested in out and about or seen clients of theirs perform. They then sent an email simply saying 'Nice to meet you …' or 'I thought X did a brilliant job ….' This approach is useful even if you don't get a response; you're preparing the ground for when you have the opportunity to make a proper approach.

Putting together your submission

Do your research, a very short email, put in a beautiful headshot …
and send it off.
                                        Successful actor and career coach

Use the guidelines over the following pages to bring all your preparation together to create an effective submission package: a short email (or in the now very unusual case, a letter), a headshot, CV and showreel if you have one.

Your submission can be sent directly to an agent or passed on if someone has offered to do so. If you are being recommended, ask if there's anything they think you should include and if you can run a draft by them. If you're on a drama course, ask for advice from and check drafts with tutors.

If you haven't already, get yourself a professional-sounding email address, add a photo and signature, and learn how to use links and send headshots (all of this is covered in Chapter 3). While almost every agent prefers online rather than mail submissions, check each agency's website for guidelines. If sending by post, type using a standard font on white or slightly tinted paper, label the reverse of your headshot with your name, include a stamped addressed envelope and put it all in an envelope with a hard back. While the rest of the advice in this section is centred around email submissions, you can apply any of the tips to a typed letter.

Agents are busy, as one told me in a weary tone, so 'don't go on too long', with another agent reassuring you don't need to include 'your whole life history' or a 'huge amount of flattery' to convince them. 'Being clear and getting to the point is valued,' a career coach explains, adding, 'they can get a lot of information and subtext in the fifteen seconds it's going to take them to read it'.

If you know the person you're writing to, let your relationship guide your tone. Most of the time of course you won't have had much or any previous contact, in which case, as one actor says, aim to find a balance between 'formality and the personal touch', with another explaining the best way to do this is by 'being yourself, but as you would in a professional environment'.

The content of your email

In the words of one industry-leading agent, addressing your email to 'All agents' or anything else vague 'looks lazy and makes it easy for your email to be deleted or ignored'. Every agent I spoke to was comfortable with actors addressing them by just their first name. Use 'Dear ...' the first time your write; only use 'Hi ...' if you know them well or they've responded to you. Sign off your email with something fairly informal like 'Many thanks' or 'Best wishes'. Avoid anything expectant ('I look forward to your response'), old-fashioned ('Awaiting your reply'), anything that suggests over-gratitude ('Thank you for your very kind consideration') ... and definitely anything too matey ('Cheers').

Between the greeting and the sign-off is where any prep you've done (pages 70–76) will come into play. Actors and agents suggest various elements you can include in your email:

Anything interesting about you and/or your current situation

Examples from interviewees include:

I am currently graduating from drama school X/university Y

I'm a recent graduate of . . .

I've just started rehearsing play Y . . .

I'm having a great time working on . . .

I've just finished performing in . . .

I'm originally from Dublin . . .

I'm a 17-year-old/60-year-old actor . . .

A reference to your recommendation or link to the agent

I believe X has already contacted you . . .

I've just been working with X and they suggested . . .

X has said nothing but great things about you . . .

I spoke to X and I think it is great what you are doing with their career . . .

For more tenuous links:

I've had an offer from agent X . . .

I'm currently meeting/talking to several agents, including X and Y . . .

I understand you saw me last year in . . .

Last year I worked with your client X . . .

I really admire your client X and what you've done for their career . . .

The ask

I'm currently looking for new representation . . .

I'm currently looking for new representation and wondering if you had any advice/would love to come in for a chat . . .

'I'm currently looking for new representation ...' and then towards the end something along the lines of, 'Any thoughts advice you have would be appreciated' or 'It would be great to come in to meet you if you have time in the next couple of weeks/when I'm back from touring/filming . . ..'

Your pitch

Your positive reason for wanting a move (e.g. go to pages 73–74) and your strengths. General strengths might include 'I've recently worked at Impressive Theatre X' or 'I'm a trained singer.' But ideally you'll tailor your strengths for each person you contact; roles that will interest that agent or suggest a casting type they don't have on their books: 'I've worked predominantly in comedy' or 'I've been cast as the Nurse in *Romeo and Juliet*.'

An invite to see your work

For plays, include the name of the show, the part, the venue, the dates and an offer to sort tickets. If you can, highlight any relevant selling points that aren't obvious (e.g. 'It's a new comedy' or 'I'm appearing alongside Well-Known Actor X'), if the show is short ('It's an hour long') and if it's convenient to get to if not a well-known venue ('... just outside Central London').

For TV, include the name of the show, the part, when it is on and what channel. If it's one or two scenes, indicate how far in you appear: 'My first appearance/my main scene is ten minutes in.' If your appearance is going to be on a catch-up service, send a link and the time at which your scene/s appear. If it's a film you're in, let them know where and when they can see it. (If they reply saying they can't catch your TV show or film screening with a positive tone, offer to send them clips once footage is released). For showreels, include a link in your email (see page 45 if you're unsure how to do this).

If you're emailing an agent you know has already seen you perform, then remind them and adapt the previous advice accordingly: for example, 'Thank you for coming to see/I understand you recently saw *Romeo and Juliet* ...'; 'X (their client) told me you'd been in to see *Romeo and Juliet* . . .'.

Combining and ordering these elements

After a polite greeting (e.g. 'How are you?', 'Hope you're well', 'It was lovely to see you at Theatre X last summer'), start with something introductory: either your current situation or a reference to your recommendation or link to the agent. From then on, prioritize the strongest elements of your approach. For example, if you have impressive previous credits then include them towards the top. But if your invite is a fantastic role in a great new show then make that one of the first things you mention.

Including CVs, photos and reels

Always include a photo, a CV and your showreel if you have one. A leading agent says you want these to be a maximum of 'one-click away', so use links wherever possible and don't send your photo as an attachment (if unsure, go to page 45 for more advice).

Sending off your submission

A leading agent told me 'I'll always make an effort to get back to anyone who writes to me personally,' and one way to increase your chances is to find an email address with the agent's name in it, rather than a general one like 'agents@...' or 'submissions@...'. Search on the agency website, go through listing guides like the *Actors and Performers Yearbook*, ask any friends you have at the agency and if you have a subscription, IMDb Pro.

For subject headings, agents suggest either name-dropping the person recommending you ('Jane Brown via John Smith'); or your name plus a couple of key selling points ('Jane Brown: Theatre X, and TV show Y regular'). If you're sending to a general submissions address like 'agents@...' then choose one of these options and include a for-attention-of and the agent's name ('FAO: Jenny Lane. Nadia Brown: Finborough Theatre, and *Doctors* regular').

Actors offer various tips if you want to be a bit strategic about the order you send off your submissions. Some recommend approaching your most realistic options first, in the hope that you'll get a meeting or an offer which you can then use to attract other agents. If you're on a drama course and feeling confident, one actor instead suggests targeting your top choices first to get you ahead of the competition. If you're feeling less sure of yourself, however, follow the strategy of another performer who told me, 'I sought out smaller agencies first to get practice at the process of meeting agents itself.'

Before finally submitting, send a version of your email to yourself to check everything's working properly. Once your submission has gone, actors advise you contact anyone who's recommended or helped you. Say thanks and let them know your email has been sent; they may even give the agent a little prompt.

Following up

'If you do it right, following up can be fine,' an agent advises, 'but don't chase hard and don't go crazy!' You may think you have nothing to lose, but the risk is being seen as pushy or desperate.

Agents' heavy schedules mean that it can take them time to reply, even if they're interested. If your submission is based solely on a show-reel, wait at least a week before thinking about sending a second email. If you've invited them to see you onscreen or stage, the same applies; leave it at least a week until after the performance has passed.

Assuming you've left a reasonable waiting time, agents say there are a few instances where it's worth following up:

- You've received an automated response saying the agent is not going to be picking up emails for an extended period (more than a few days). Check in closer to your showcasing opportunity when they're back online

- You've contacted an agent way in advance of your showcase performance. Send an informal reminder a few days before

- You've been recommended by someone the agent knows. Ask for advice; they may check in with the agent for you

- You have a good previous relationship with the agent (you've had emails back and forth before). Send a brief reminder closer to the date of your showcasing opportunity

- You've since received an offer from another agent

- Your invite was to see you onscreen. Send some clips of your appearance

Agent meetings

You're aiming to have a conversation.
                                        Experienced stage and screen performer

If an agent is interested in your submission, you'll be invited for a meeting. Usually this will be a chat at the agent's office and last between 15 and 30 minutes (a very small minority of actors I spoke to had been asked to perform at a meeting).

A leading agent explains a meeting normally has three main aims: 'to see if we like you, essentially, whether we can work with you; to get a better understanding of what you have laid out in your submission; and (to learn more about) your potential employability and how we will be presented through you at auditions'. For actors, the aims are simple: make a good impression and gather information to help make a decision if offered representation.

General preparation for a meeting

The advice on what to wear is simple. 'Don't treat it like a job interview; don't wear anything formal like a suit,' an agent outlines. Instead, pick out things from your everyday wardrobe that are 'clean and presentable'.

Pre-meeting nerves are normal so, as one actor says, if you get a few butterflies, 'don't fight it feeling weird'. Quickly reminding yourself of your selling points will boost your confidence. And, as a recent graduate suggests, remember 'they've brought you in because they think you could potentially fill a gap and add value to their list'. An actor who's been through several meetings meanwhile says, 'it's worth remembering that a lot of it is out of your hands and they're thinking about your age, physique, look and casting as much as anything else', with another actor putting things more bluntly: 'I feel the agent chooses you and there's not a hell of a lot you can do about it.' Rather than fixate on the result of your meeting, it can be freeing to accept that all you can really do is prepare, turn up on time and see what happens.

Talking points in a meeting

Actors and agents agree that meetings should feel like a chat rather than a formal job interview, and there are various ways you can create the right tone. Being indirect is often advised, with a leading agent explaining, 'Don't say "Are you an expert in theatre or TV?" ... if you want to find this out, talk about the industry with them.' They add that asking for advice is also a good strategy: 'Rather than say, "What do you see my casting as?" – which might make them feel like they're being tested – say something like, "I feel I could be in several casting categories; what do you think would be most useful for me to position myself in?" '

Actors suggest you gently think about and research likely conversational topics. To help you be (or at least appear to be) natural, have these in your back pocket rather than come up with set questions and answers. As one actor explains, 'a meeting is more instinctive than that, and it's difficult to fully prepare because until you're in there you can't gauge what's right'.

In the days before, think about or remind yourself of:

- Your positive reason/s for approaching the agent
- Details of your CV: where you worked, with whom, and the parts you played
- Your other selling points, especially your casting types
- Casting directors, producers or directors you've auditioned for or have met in the industry
- The agent and agency's client list
- Theatre, TV and film you have seen recently
- Your favourite actors, actors who've had a similar career to you or are where you want to head next, and who's who around your career level and in the industry generally

Below are listed common talking points:

The agent and the agency

Actors say this is a good way to break the ice and ease yourself into the meeting.

Sample questions include: 'How did you become an agent?'; 'Are there commercials or voice-over departments at the agency?'

Preferred working styles

If the agent doesn't go into how they like to do things, you can ask, especially if you have specific needs to address. If you're meeting a top-level agent, it's important you consider their status; some won't expect their clients to be using casting sites or regularly making audition suggestions.

Sample question: 'Do you like your new clients to get in touch with casting directors?'

Their client list

A leading career coach recommends 'talking to them about a specific client that they look after. This will flatter the agent, show you've done some research, that you take an interest in the industry and a specific interest in that agent.' This is also useful for getting a sense of the type of auditions and work they get for their clients, their passion and commitment, and where you might fit in to their list.

If you've been recommended by a client then ask about them. If not, another agent interviewed advises, 'mention if you have worked with or know a client; you'll look good through association'. Alternatively, ask about someone working at a similar level to you or whose trajectory you could potentially follow.

Sample questions/comments: 'I had a brilliant time working with X recently'; 'I really admire Y. How long have you been working with them?'

Your aims

While an agent can't guarantee you results, you should both be on the same page when it comes to what you want from your career. A top agent has some tips: 'Don't walk in the room and say "All I'm interested in doing is feature films." That shows a lack of versatility and it is unrealistic; and that you probably don't want to be an actor for any other reason than chasing fame and fortune.' They add that if an agent suggests work that's a realistic possibility, you should 'never rule anything out'.

An actor points out: 'the questions that you want to ask might feel quite awkward. Essentially you want to know, "Can you get me an audition for the RSC?"' Their advice is to take an indirect approach instead and start a conversation by talking about the casting directors, directors, actors, types of shows, venues and companies that you are interested in, and why. An alternative option here is to 'ask them what they think is realistic', says one experienced performer. And another explains that if you feel it's important to be ambitious, 'phrase it as "In the long term . . ."'

Sample comments/questions: 'I have a bit of experience in TV/theatre/comedy/drama, but would like to explore more'; 'What do you think is realistic, given my current credits?'

Your casting

As with other areas, be open to their ideas about your casting, while offering something yourself. An experienced TV actor says, 'it's important to be honest about what you want and let your love for what you do be evident. If you are good at a particular thing, like comedy, you should mention that.' To talk about your casting more indirectly, discuss the type of work and actors you're interested in that cover your brackets.

Sample questions/comments: 'I've played role X recently which I really enjoyed'; 'I've been occasionally been seen for casting bracket X and would love to do more of that'; 'Are there any casting brackets you think I should be focusing on/new brackets I could be exploring?'

Your strengths

An actor highlights the importance of giving 'a sense of what you can offer (an agent) in return for representation', while another says 'you'll never find a successful salesperson saying "I have this product. I hope you like it. I think it's kinda good."'

Sample comments/questions: 'I'm fluent in German'; 'That role was great to work on because I got to use my German'; 'Are there ways I could make more use of my language skills?'

Discussing your current agent

As mentioned already, the advice here, as one actor describes, is 'to speak very respectfully of the agent you are leaving. If they like you as an actor but you come in mouthing off about another agent they might think you are difficult.'

Sample comments/questions: 'I really enjoyed aspects of working with my previous agent, but I'd really like an agent who can help me with . . .'

Your industry general knowledge and awareness

One leading agent reveals that 'many actors don't seem to be knowledgeable about the industry, they don't show passion or interest for it. This is odd! Real knowledge of theatre, TV and film will really turn an agent on,' with others adding it will also spark conversation, help you pick up threads, build rapport and inform you about their tastes.

Sample comments/questions: 'I recently saw X and thought it was fantastic …'; 'Did you see theatre company X/TV show Y recently?'

Other agents you've applied to, are meeting and had offers from

If an agent says something like 'I'm sure you are meeting other people,' then mention any relatively impressive names you can. If not, then actors suggest answering with a vague nod or a 'Yes', listing agents you met when you last applied for representation (e.g. 'I met X as I was coming out of drama school last year'), or saying you're trying to set up meetings with a couple of the names you've applied to.

Anything unusual about your current situation

It may be that you have a busy second career or you live miles away from where a prospective agent is based. If you've had problems with a previous agent about an aspect of your situation, or it's something you want out in the open from the start, then the time to gently bring it up is during the meeting.

Your interests outside of acting

Finally, one actor reveals that an agent asked what they liked to do outside of performing: 'I was a bit stumped by it … I hadn't thought about or prepared anything other than bigging up my acting.' While this topic doesn't always come up, it's worth having a think about so you're not left um-ing and ah-ing.

Offers

There is nothing wrong with saying that you'd like to go away and think about it.

Leading agent

An offer of representation may come in the meeting itself, in which case you can accept there and then, or in the days afterwards. But if you have some doubts or are waiting for other offers, take some time. Agents say as long as you keep them up to date, a clear verbal offer stands for as long as the actor needs to make the decision. One I spoke to adds that drama students especially 'shouldn't fall in to the trap of, "We can only keep this offer open for two weeks." This is bullshit. Everyone knows the process, and if they want you, they want you.' If you're on a course and in this situation, talk to your course staff.

Saying goodbye to your current agent

If you've accepted an offer and you're already represented, the next step is to say goodbye to your previous agent. Agents are pretty clear that you shouldn't send an email, with one saying 'it's like being dumped by text'. Phoning is considered the least stressful option by most actors interviewed. However, one suggests: 'if you've had a long, good relationship with the agent you could go in and do it face to face … if you can bear it and you think it is going to be alright'. Actors who had a close relationship suggest that after speaking to the agent, send a card and/or gift to say thank you properly, and email saying thank you to other people in the office.

While your old agent may well be understanding, there were several stories from actors where what should have been a professional discussion turned into a messy break up, and it's worth being prepared for your agent to become emotional and fight to keep you.

An area you can easily trip up is explaining your decision. As an agent highlights, 'often you just want a better agent … Well, it's very difficult to tell someone that'. Their advice is to avoid sounding accusatory and keep your reason vague: 'Something like, "It's nothing personal, but with my last job, I think now is the right time for me to make a change," or "I think now is a good time to try something new."' If you face objections, acknowledge the agent's frustrations with a gentle apology and repeat your reasons why. 'Remain professional!' says an actor who went through a tricky conversation. They and many others say be sensitive to the fact that this may be difficult for an agent; they may be shocked by the news, have lost other clients recently or be frustrated because they've put time, money and effort into your career and want to see it pay off.

Finally, one actor who had recently made a successful move has advice on how to stay strong: 'Remember what you are aiming for (in your career). Remember it is business. Remember you have made your old agent money. And remember that lots of people will have been through this. Be prepared to feel guilty and for the agent to get pissy with you; you don't want to let this spoil the enjoyment of your move.'

Getting a 'No' at any point in the process

It's fine, I'm so used to it, who gives a shit.
                        Actor, with more than one agent email in their sent box

Normally, if an agent is unable to see you for a meeting or take you on, it's simply a case that you won't hear back from them. But if at any point you do get a reply with a 'No', follow the advice from one cool-headed actor who says, 'don't beg, keep your dignity and be ready to strike another day. Send a quick email back saying thank you, and if they ask you to stay in touch acknowledge that as well.'

While coping with knock-backs isn't easy, as one actor empha-sizes, 'unfortunately rejection is part of the profession and if you can't find ways to deal with it then it can seep out in your auditions, perfor-mances, emails and meetings'. Luckily, there are some tips from actors and agents to help.

Hold on to as much perspective as you can (as one career coach highlights, 'agents turn so many down and you have to be lucky') and remember the reasons why or why not are largely beyond your control. Agents say it can simply be that their list is very full at the moment, your casting clashes with another of their clients, you don't as yet have quite the right experience level, they don't think they are currently able to help you with what you're aiming for or they like you but haven't seen enough of your work yet.

While of course it's natural to wallow for a while, try to see the posi-tives. A non-response isn't rudeness on their part; an assistant I spoke to underlines that even if they've read your email, agents are busy and unfortunately 'it is impossible to write back to everyone', adding reassuringly, 'they may well have taken notice of you and your name'. Several agents and actors point out that you may soon find yourself in a better position, with one experienced actor advising you think of your first contact as 'priming'. They explain, 'a "No" may be a connection that you can take advantage of in the future. The next time you've got a show to invite them to … well great, 'cos you've already made that first contact.' Meanwhile, one now-successful actor says if you don't land your ideal agent straight away, 'over the course of your career you can hop up the agent ladder. It is quite normal to start small and work your way up'.

Finally, it's important to remember that getting an agent isn't the be-all and end-all, with some actors interviewed admitting that at times they'd become detrimentally fixated on finding new representation. Realizing that an agent is just one factor in a successful career will take off some of the pressure and get your attention and energy going towards things you can control. In fact, several interviewees point out that focusing on your current agent (if already represented), other ways of finding work and getting better as a performer are the things that will eventually lead you to the representation you're chasing.

Going again

Advice suggests that you should leave at least a few months before reapplying to the same agents; otherwise you may be seen as a nuisance and undo any good work resulting from your original email. 'You need to be in a new, strong position,' explains one actor, meaning you'll need a new showcase opportunity of the right level. The only real exception to this – as was the case for a couple of actor-interviewees – is if you've come very close to signing, but the agent has said they need to see more of you. In this case, consider inviting them to any sort of showcasing opportunity in which you're happy with your performance, however soon; it may clinch the deal.

To help you judge the right time to make a new approach, keep a record of who you've already contacted, when you emailed them and any responses. Agents move around a lot between agencies, and assistants and associates get promoted and start their own lists; keep tabs on what's happening generally and you might spot opportunities for next time.

It's also worth assessing if there's anything you could do better going forward. Did you target the right level of agents or did you aim too high? Was your email brief, and did it properly highlight your

strengths? Did you go in cold, or did you have links and recommendations to help you? Could your photo and/or showreel be improved?
Could you have made it easier for them to attend your show or see
your onscreen appearance? Did you get your submission in on time?
Work on anything you can while you wait for your next opportunity
to submit.

*For free resources to help you make the most of the expert advice
in this chapter, visit www.actorscareerbible.com/freestuff*

7

BUILDING THE RELATIONSHIP WITH YOUR AGENT

'In a business partnership, you wouldn't expect to do all the work and let your partner sit there twiddling their thumbs, and I think the same is true for the actor–agent relationship.' This view from one actor was shared by many other interviewees, including every agent I spoke to. As another performer bluntly puts it, 'it's crazy to spend three years training, and then hand your whole career over to an absolute stranger and say, "You deal with it now, and if you don't get me any auditions then the failure of my career is your fault." You've got to get off your arse and get things done!' This chapter will take you through advice on four key areas of the relationship you can work on, moving you closer, as one actor exclaims, to 'a satisfying sense of partnership!'

Use the advice in this chapter to work on:

- Communicating effectively with your agent
- Maintaining a useful attitude
- Making yourself easy to promote
- Adopting the right level of self-marketing

Communicate effectively with your agent

Never ring up without something to give or tell them that is positive and conducive to your succeeding as an actor.

Experienced agent

For many actors interviewed, applying normal social skills and a bit of professional etiquette is enough to ensure communication with their agent occurs fairly freely. However, several I spoke to had faced problems: agents they felt were impatient and negative; agents who were unwilling to address problems; being fobbed off to an assistant; or a complete communication black hole. If you're dealing with something similar, all you can control is your own behaviour, so use this section to make sure you're regularly doing the right things.

Balance your preferences with theirs

Recognizing your agent's preferences is important in building your relationship. For instance, do they prefer regular contact or are they more hands-off? Do they like lots of personal chit-chat or do they keep things strictly professional? Are they encouraging when it comes to you suggesting auditions, discussing submissions and self-marketing, or do those sorts of things feel unnecessary or inappropriate?

Equally, think about how you work best. For example, do you prefer an informal, matey relationship or something more business-like? Do you want to work closely alongside your agent or just let them get on with things? How much contact do you need to reassure you the relationship is bubbling along?

The key is to find a balance that works for both of you, compromising where necessary. You can discuss both of your particular preferences with them directly if it feels appropriate; otherwise, slowly introduce any habits you want to establish. The earlier you do this the better; as one actor explains, if you never speak on the phone in the first few months, 'it will become an event when later down the line you do ring up'.

Find the right amount of contact

While advice like 'trust your agent is working hard for you' and 'don't hassle them' was common, interviewees were keen to point out that breaking silences with your agent once in a while has benefits beyond helping you feel reassured. Actors say it's through both chit-chat and industry-related back-and-forth that a rapport is created, and, as one career coach advises, it's important to 'keep yourself near the forefront of your agent's mind, in a good way. Remind them of your presence, give them a nudge. They can only think about so many actors at one time.'

There are two key things to avoid when thinking about initiating contact. First, prevent over-communicating by resisting using your agent as a shoulder to cry on. A leading agent reveals, 'there's nothing worse than a needy actor. Reassurance is fine sometimes; the actor can offload a little bit and it wouldn't be weird. But we don't want a sob story every day. An actor should probably use an agent in this role as a last resort, or when things are positive (e.g. just missing out on a big role).' Second, be wary of under-communicating because you're intimidated by your agent. As one actor highlights, 'a healthy relationship is one where you feel you can speak to them openly and honestly. You don't want that monkey on your back: a block between you and them.' Another actor outlines the mindset to adopt: 'as useful as they are for you, you have to believe you are useful for them'.

Beyond those two key points, a career coach says 'as long as you contact them for a good reason, most modern agents will be pleased you're doing something to help them do their job'. The following list gives all the good, occasional and bad reasons for initiating contact suggested by interviewees. Check this list whenever you're going through a quiet period and feeling unsure (there is further advice on many of these points later in this chapter):

Good reasons for initiating contact:

- Updates on your limited availability
- For advice on marketing materials
- Admin around auditions and jobs (check emails yourself carefully first)
- Invites to see your work
- Organizing tickets for them to see your show
- If you have a major problem on jobs
- Pay-related problems. Bring these up with your agent or the agency's accounts department
- Changes to your contact details or a major change in your situation

Occasional reasons, or reasons depending on your relationship:

- Realistic new ambitions
- Audition suggestions
- Self-marketing updates
- Calling or emailing after an audition. The if-in-doubt advice is to be gently positive: for example, 'Was nice to meet them … enjoyed it … see what happens … thanks for the meeting'. If you're comfortable enough then the occasional small moan is ok: for example, you genuinely feel something was unfair in the room, or for once (!) you didn't nail it
- Finding out about audition results. Always give a reasonable waiting time (normally at least a week)
- Following up something you've asked them about: for example, an audition suggestion
- Occasional updates when you're on a job: for example, how much you're enjoying it
- Asking if there is anything extra you could be doing during quiet periods
- Discussing a problem in the relationship
- Asking to come in to see them
- Thanking them for something
- Congratulating them on their news: for example, a promotion or, if you're close, something in their personal life

Reasons to avoid:

- Moaning about a problem you haven't addressed yourself yet
- Complaining about a lack of auditions without something constructive to say
- Demanding to know what you've been submitted for or why you haven't been submitted for a particular project
- Asking something vague about auditions like, 'What is happening?' or 'What's out there at the moment?'

- In most cases, asking for audition feedback. An agent explains: 'We can call up and ask "Why?" to casting directors ... but it's a bit pointless because the casting director will just say, "Well, we found someone more suitable"'

- Checking up or following up on something without a reasonable time for them to act on it and get back to you

- Complaining, panicking or offloading about the industry or current state of your career

- Calling up with lots of personal heavy stuff, especially with a relatively new agent

- Suggesting changes to your marketing because you're panicking: for example, replacing perfectly good photos or drastically changing your whole look

Going in to see your agent

Most actors interviewed advise waiting to be invited in to see your agent or picking your moments. A commonly suggested reason for going in is to address major problems, but a sunny actor recommends something more positive: when you're working and things are going well, 'touch base, and spread a bit of good cheer'. Others suggest arranging a meeting at the end of a longish job, to catch up and plan some next moves. And many actors advise asking to go in simply because you haven't seen your agent in a while. As one highlights, this is especially useful 'if you look different, for example, if you've got yourself into shape', with another saying, 'I think it's important, otherwise they just have an old headshot and your voice over the phone. My agent said, "It's great that you've come in. You look different to how you looked two years ago!"'

Depending on your relationship, you don't have to just go into their office. A leading agent suggests, 'every so often say to them, "Do you want to go out for a quick bite to eat at lunch?" Keep it informal; pop to Pizza Express or something every now and then.' Some actors I spoke to go to see shows with their agent, and even out and about for dinner or drinks.

Whatever your reason, a top agent warns, 'Face-to-face time is good, but don't turn up unannounced because that will just piss an agent off. They are really busy. Always ask and give a few days' notice … and present yourself like you would for a casting!'

Gifts and kindnesses

Lots of actor-interviewees drop off cards or small gifts to their agent, at Christmas, if they get a big job or to celebrate the agent's achievements, with one actor saying, 'when my agent moved in to her new office and stopped being an associate, I took a bottle of champagne in'.

As one performer explains, 'yes, they have a bunch of clients and you've only got one agent but, like in any other walk of life, if your social skills are interchangeable rather than one way, it's going to make people want to spend time with you, and want to work hard for you.' The only warning here comes from one performer who says 'don't buy things just to be a kiss-ass'.

Troubleshooting with agents

Throughout this chapter is advice on the most common representation-related problems. The problem-solving steps involved are outlined below, which you can apply to any other issues in the relationship.

Step 1: Decide if the problem really needs addressing.

Develop realistic expectations, learn to trust your agent and let the small things and one-offs go. If something does come up, see if you can deal with it yourself first. Give some time (more than just a few weeks) to see if your increased efforts have an effect.

Step 2: Get yourself in a good place.

As a career coach explains, 'if you're contacting them from a place of frustration, then that's only going to result in irritation from one side or the other'.

Step 3: Bring up the problem.

Whether you decide to use email or call them up, controlling your tone is key; aim to be assertive rather than accusatory. Offering solutions will also help your cause; if you can't think of solutions to suggest, ask your agent for their thoughts on what you could be doing to solve the problem.

Step 4: Try the solutions … and give it time

It may take a few months for you to see any progress.

If after trying these four steps there's still no change, then interviewees suggest three options: assuming other parts of the relationship are working, accept the problem; go through this four-step process again, this time being more direct with your own efforts, asking for a meeting and being clearer about new solutions; if the problem is recurring and holding you back then consider seeking new representation.

Maintain a useful attitude

A negative approach doesn't serve anyone.
Industry leading agent

As highlighted earlier in this chapter, your relationship with your agent will work best if you see it as a partnership; this section shares advice on further ways to create a useful attitude.

Get to know your agent and agency

Actors advise you take an interest in who works at your agency, with one emphasizing, 'know who the assistants are and ask about them … know who the accountant is and ask about them!' Several actors highlighted the value of building relationships with assistants, with one admitting, 'my agent's assistant is less intimidating and easier to connect with', adding that they may be submitting you for certain jobs, and importantly 'often go on to have their own lists'.

Actors also advise you familiarize yourself with your agent's client list. This will give you a clearer idea of the type of work your agent is interested in and potential avenues for you to explore.

Develop realistic audition expectations

A career coach reveals that from their experience of working with hundreds of performers, 'what an actor thinks should be the frequency of their castings is often quite unrealistic'. Their advice, echoed by many others, is that before you leap to blame your agent during slow periods, you should first develop accurate expectations: 'Otherwise you will build up frustration that will only hinder you.'

To do this, you need to avoid two common mistakes. The first is basing your expectations solely on the reputation of your agent. There is a very general link between the reputation of the agent/agency and the amount of auditions an actor gets. However, it's important to understand this only gives a rough sense of what to expect, and there are many exceptions. Some actors I spoke to with big name agents don't get seen for months, and a few actors with agents you might have never heard of get regular meetings. The point is there are many factors beyond the reputation of your agent that affect your audition rate, and you have to bear these in mind when making a judgement:

- Your availability

- Your own marketing efforts

- Your previous experience. 'If you don't have that credit and no footage on your showreel, then you are not necessarily going to get in the door for a major role on a TV series', a casting director highlights

- Your casting types. You may get very few auditions because you're in a very competitive bracket, or as one successful actor reveals, a very narrow one: 'I'm simply not an actor who gets lots of auditions. If you're a very specific physical type then that might be the case for you'

- Your existing industry relationships. For some 'self-propelling actors', as one agent calls them, a lot of the work comes to them because of strong ties in the industry built through regularly working with the same people

- Changing trends in the industry. 'There are a cycle of things that are sought after for casting, like (types of) looks or accents,' one agent observes

- The time of year. An agent outlines how this can effect television casting: 'Christmas is dead ... then at the end of January, Americans wake up and get everything together for pilot season. There's a frenzy of activity here and in the United States, and UK TV is also strong at this time of year. That can last until the end of

April ... then at Easter there is a dip ... it kicks back in towards the summer and dies off towards the end of July ... then it all picks back up again mid-September. So, if it's quiet, that may just be the nature of the business; not because your agent has forgotten about you'

- Where you are in your relationship with the agent. A career-coach outlines how your expectations can be inflated by a surge of auditions when you first sign: 'Agents want to find out where their client is successful. Do you meet casting directors well, do you do well on tape, are you good for commercials? That can peter out a bit.' An experienced actor explains that the opposite can happen; a disappointingly slow period when you sign while they get to know you and get your name out there: 'There's always a period of adjustment that should be allowed for'

The second common mistake to be aware of is comparing your audition rate with people in completely different casting brackets, with more experience or a higher level of agent than you currently have. As one seasoned actor observes, this can particularly be a problem for final year students and very recent graduates: 'It's understandable they don't take a long-term view. They feel pressure to get off to a flying start because of the success of one person in their year, and think, "I'm already failing in the business and I haven't even been out for a year!"'

Avoid these traps and instead aim for an idea of a vague average over an extended period. Always consider how various factors might be currently effecting your rate. And only compare yourself with friends and colleagues of similar casting and experience. Becoming more widely aware of who's getting cast in what will also help; if the roles you want to be seen for all go to actors with more impressive credits than you or the one or two bright young things graduating each year, then your expectations are probably too high for now.

Realistic expectations – and an acceptance that quiet periods are inevitable for every actor – will help you keep a level head during the odd slow spell. And as one experienced actor advises, rather than turn on your agent, 'if you're honest with yourself you might think, "My credits aren't strong enough to attract the next level up, and where I am at the moment is of the right level." If you want to move up to a higher level of agent then your prospects and credits need to reflect that potential; that should be where you put your focus.'

If you genuinely think you're going through an unusually extended quiet period and you're not happy, experienced actors and agents suggest using the four steps listed on pages 96–97. Acknowledge the problem gently: something indirect like, 'I realize things are a bit slow at the moment,' an actor suggests. Then ask for solutions. Actors again recommend being indirect: 'Is there anything I could be doing to help?' or 'Is there a reason you think I'm not getting seen?'

Focus on the positives

While you shouldn't be complacent if there's a genuine problem to address, try to appreciate your agent's *range* of qualities whenever you can. As one successful screen performer says, 'it's a natural state for an actor to moan about their agent, but you diminish your power every time you do; try being grateful instead'.

One actor I spoke to acknowledges they might get one or two more auditions with another agent, but says, 'I feel they believe in me, and they've really stood by me when I haven't been working.' Another says proudly, 'I trust them and I'm not scared of them. We have a connection and are on the same level; crucial if you want things between you to be plain-sailing.' One actor interviewed highlights, 'agents will do the shitty things that need doing but you are too scared to do. They will serve you better than you can serve yourself and are prepared to do for your career what you are not.' And a performer-turned-agent says, 'a good agent will work their socks off for you. Getting you seen by a casting director may be a long process and they do a lot of other stuff for you besides getting you auditions. Give them respect, it's hard work.'

Control any fears of getting dropped

The range of agents I spoke to were keen to limit actor's fears about being let go. One told me, 'an agent will only sign you if they know what they want to and can do with you. You have to take confidence from this', while another highlights, 'an agent's joy and hope is that when they take on an actor, they are there for a long time. It's an exciting journey which you are going to be a part of together'.

Agents say they like to give actors time: 'We understand the pressure actors are under.' They point out that most agents aren't in a position where they need to drop clients: 'If your list is small enough then you can handle people not working.' And even if it does get to a point where an agent feels they can't work with a client any longer, they reveal 'most would prefer to keep an actor on their list and put them up for things now. It is a stressful process dropping someone.'

If a client is ever let go, agents say there's always a good reason: 'It's because the relationship is not working: there's no communication or the relationship is unhappy.' And they argue that if it does happen, its often the best thing: 'The alternative is that you'd be sat dormant on a list, which is worse. You're better off being dropped and looking for a new agent.' One actor I spoke to about this reveals, 'my relationship breakdown with my agent lasted over a year! Your agent might not push you to leave and you may be hanging around for ages waiting, so, if you're sure, make the first move and get out of there. You'll then be approaching new agents from a position of power.'

Make yourself easy to promote

You shouldn't wait and let someone else be responsible for your career. You should be working just as hard as they are to bring in work.

Experienced career coach

Interviewees offer lots of simple ways to make your agent's jobs easier, keeping them happy and increasing your chances of getting a casting.

Be available … and keep them up to date

As one agent underlines, if you're given a meeting, 'there's an expectation that you'll cancel everything'. They explain you should be flexible enough to attend auditions during the working week and find time to prepare for auditions on weeknights and weekends. Agents also expect you to receive and respond to their calls and emails promptly.

If you have got something coming up, as one actor advises, 'being upfront with them will make your life much easier'. Actors and agents give instances of when you can legitimately say you're going to be unavailable:

- Holidays and trips coming up (though an agent might still expect you to be available to self-tape)

- Major family and friend events, like a wedding

- Auditions or work via other agencies (for example, commercials or voiceover) and other acting-related business (for example, a headshot session or a showreel edit)

- If you're too ill to audition or have a medical appointment

- Reasonable second job schedule issues (one interviewee let their agent know they couldn't audition past 5 pm because of an evening job)

Work on your selling points

The greater quality and range of your strengths, the easier for your agent to get you seen for auditions. Agents and career coaches encourage actors to take responsibility for this; see Chapter 1 to go through your selling points. Another key aspect of your employability is your mental state, especially during longer periods out of work. Giving off a sense of vitality, enthusiasm and confidence (even if you're faking it) is going to serve you better at auditions than a general air of despair; go to Chapter 13 for more advice.

If you have been busying away with self-improvement, a career coach advises, 'update your agent every month or so. Let them know any new skills you've learnt, people you have worked with, things you've seen that you would like to be considered for and anyone you've contacted; anything that enhances your saleability and castability.' This career coach acknowledges it might not feel appropriate in every relationship, especially if you're represented by a big name. However, for most actors they say there's probably no harm in sending an update email, especially if things are quiet.

Align your goals with your agent

'You want to make your goals congruent with that of your agent,' one actor says sensibly, and the general advice is to talk to them about genres, mediums, size of roles and the level of productions you're interested in, over the short and longer term. The key thing here is to offer realistic ideas based on your previous experience; as one agent warns, 'don't just tell them "I want to be a movie star!"'

A busy actor advises to be specific: 'Tell them five or six things that you want to do. Or say something like, "If there is one meeting I really want this year then it's …"'. You also can be honest about what you don't want to do. As one actor points out, 'if you are going up for loads of jobs that you don't particularly want, the likelihood is that you won't get most of them'.

It's equally important to find out what your agent thinks, with one experienced performer suggesting you ask, 'What do you think is realistic right now?' And a successful actor-producer advises, 'ask your agent not only what goals you should be working towards but *what you should be doing* to work towards them'.

You can also cover goals in less direct ways, such as a bit of chit-chat over the phone or as an extra paragraph in an email: let your agent know if there are actors or shows you've recently seen and loved; ask them about shows and work they like and have seen; and if you work on your own projects, keep them up to date with how they're progressing.

Good times to update your agent on your latest aims include:

- When you first sign. Several actors suggest sending a new agent a list of casting directors and other people in the industry you've auditioned for, worked with or have ties to

- At the beginning of and during a job as you plan invites for people in the industry

- At the end of the job as you get ready to become available again

- If you're going through an extended slow period

Involve your agent in your marketing decisions

As one career coach urges, 'use your agent's expertise!' This could be about anything from headshot and showreel choices to getting into specialist areas like voiceover. This will help you with your aims, is a sensible use of their time and an easy way to have some contact with them.

Give your best to auditions

Simple advice, but giving your all to every audition was often mentioned as the top way to build the relationship with your agent; increasing your chances of working and making them look good in front of casting teams. Make sure you have the resources, skills and confidence you need in place to audition at a moment's notice, and check you aren't making avoidable mistakes on the day; go to Part Three of this guide for tips.

Encourage them to see your work

'If you're doing professional work that you're proud of, really push your agent to come and bring people with them to see it,' urges one career coach. Unfortunately, according to actors interviewed, not every agent is a willing audience member. The advice is that if you think your agent needs a little prompting, take the initiative by sending them an invite-email or calling them up. This also applies to their bringing industry people to see you. If you're concerned (or just want to be a bit proactive) ask them which casting directors might be interested, or as an experienced actor suggests, 'email over a short, well-researched list'.

Agents explain that sometimes they will have legitimate reasons for saying 'No'; if their schedule is booked up, the show is miles away from their office or it's a tiny role or at a level way below what you normally do. However, if you think it's important they see it, it's always worth asking; actors gave plenty of examples of big name agents making things at very short notice, travelling across the country and coming to see them play walk-on roles and even parts in readings.

Alternatively, one actor suggests 'asking if one of their assistants or associates would be interested'. And whether your agent comes or not, a career coach says, 'always find out who's been in from the industry to see you and let your agent know'. (Pick up this information by checking at the box office and by asking around other actors in the cast.)

Any performance you can get them along to is going to be beneficial, but many actors advise inviting your agent to an opening night; it's more fun for them, it's easier to get casting directors along and, as one performer explains, 'they can help you mingle with audience from the industry'.

If you're appearing on TV, the advice is to send a short email reminder in the days before your show is going to be on. A top agent suggests you can also 'send clips straight after the show has aired. The next day I can then send it out to casting directors who might have missed it: "X was in this great show last night, here's some cut scenes from it."'

Making audition suggestions

Several actors with higher level agents advise against making audition suggestions. As one performer explains, 'you have to have a clear understanding of the work your agent is doing for you. If you are represented by one of the big players, do you really go in and say, "Can you put me up for this?"' Another successful actor reveals, 'I've done it when I've been out of work for a while, when there are projects going on that I feel I should be seen for. Usually the response is, "We put you up for it but you are the wrong age-bracket" or "They are looking for a Chinese person". To be honest, I often feel it just undermines them a bit.'

However, the advice for most actors is you should feel confident making the odd sensible suggestion when things are quiet. As one agent says, 'if you think you're right for the role, don't be scared. You should feel like you have a relationship where you can drop them an email without feeling they're going to bite your head off.' They add that the 'sensible' aspect is key: 'Don't suggest yourself for blindingly obvious things. Keep suggestions reflective of where you are in your career; you're not going to be considered for the lead role on the next Working Title movie if you've done nothing before. And be specific. Don't ring up just to say, "I want to be at The National" or "What is happening?" That will just annoy your agent.' Research is your main weapon here; use the advice in Chapter 2 to find castings and check your suggestions.

Be informal and brief in your email, but within that give your agent as many details as you can: the role, where it's on, who's casting it, what they're looking for and why you might be suitable. One actor adds, 'always

offer them something as well: "I've just written this email to so and so …
can I get seen for this?"' If you're unsure, take the edge of a request by
couching it in a less direct question. An agent suggests something like, '"I
saw X the other day at the theatre. I really liked it, and I know Y is coming
up that's similar. Is that the sort of thing I could be considered for?"', while
an actor suggests asking for advice: '"I know X is being cast – what work
do I have to do to be considered for that type of thing in the future?"'

Make a decision about discussing submissions

While one experienced agent I spoke to is positive about actors bringing up submissions ('don't be afraid to ask what you're being put up
for'), most say be careful, warning that if misjudged it can seem like
you're checking up on them. One agent explains, 'they will almost definitely have submitted you for a job if you're right. They are not trying to
teach you a lesson. Ultimately, they want you to do well, and they also
want to make money out of you!'

To discuss submissions, give goal-setting (as opposed to checking
up on them!) as your reason why. And, as one agent's assistant advises,
manage your tone: 'Don't call up and say, "Why haven't I been seen for
this!?" Don't blame them! "Is there a particular reason they didn't want
to see me?" is better.'

Adopt the right level of self-marketing

*Different behaviour and pushing is appropriate for different levels
of agent.*
                    Experienced and successful theatre and screen actor

'Self-marketing' refers to your efforts to find work outside of everything
your agent does. There's lots of basic stuff you can do that's largely your
responsibility and is beneficial whatever your career-stage:

- Keeping your marketing materials up to date (photos, CVs and
  showreels)

- Updating your online marketing: for example, the latest news on
  your website or Twitter bio

- Following and engaging with industry-related people on Twitter and other social media
- Keeping on top of your selling points
- Doing a bit of networking: getting out and about at industry-related events
- Using direct contact and social media to stay in touch with people you've worked with and are close to
- Keeping tabs on what's going on in the industry

Beyond that, there are more proactive things you can do. Examples of heavier self-marketing include:

- Using direct contact to get in touch with industry figures you don't yet know
- Applying for jobs through direct contact (firing off emails to casting directors) or casting sites
- Pushier networking

Aim for a level of this heavier self-marketing that suits both you and your agent, a balance between not treading on their toes and not leaving everything in their hands. Among the actors I spoke to, there are a few different approaches:

Very limited/no heavy self-marketing

Beyond the absolute basics, leave everything in your agent's control. Actors suggest you take this approach if: you're already getting enough auditions; you trust your agent to submit you for anything suitable; you're with a bigger name agent and feel heavy self-marketing isn't appropriate; you're focusing on other priorities, for example being audition-ready or making money from your second job.

Self-market closely alongside your agent

One experienced agent I spoke to is particularly keen on this approach, saying: 'I like to work in conjunction with the client. It's more powerful ... you do what you can to get that audition.' They give an example: 'If you've heard that a particular casting director is casting a show, ask your agent if it would help for you to drop them a line as well. Your agent might say "Not this time", but they might say "Absolutely". You can then email saying "I know my agent has mentioned me for this role ... I just wanted to say hello as well ... at the moment I'm doing this, this and this . . ."'

An actor who benefits from this tandem approach describes how it works for them: 'In quiet seasons, I write to casting directors or people I've worked with in the past to see what future work is coming up they might consider me for, and my agent then backs me up with a following call or email.' Another describes how they do things: 'I ask what the latest is for shows I'm passionate about, I let my agent know what I've heard from my mates, and every time I email someone I let them know and ask, "Can you contact them?"'

All of this of course is dependent on you asking your agent and receiving the go-ahead, and then working on a case-by-case basis. While one successful actor exclaims 'push your agent!', most recommend being sensitive to how they like to operate.

Having sought your agent's blessing, do your own thing

Your agent may be happy to let you get on with things by yourself. As one actor explains, 'if you ask about emailing casting directors and directors, most agents will say, "As long as it's professional and sensible."' If you're given free rein, gently involve your agent every so often by sending an update email with who you've contacted and any replies.

What to do if you're being restricted by your agent

One agent emphasizes there are legitimate reasons why less is sometimes more when it comes to actor self-marketing: 'It depends; you have to choose carefully who and when. Some casting directors really respond to it, some don't. You can do too much; it is good to nudge, but you don't want to nag. And at times it might be more powerful if the agent just does it and the actor doesn't; you can keep a bit of mystery back about that client.'

What's problematic is if your agent is consistently very controlling about your self-marketing and can't give you a good reason. As one actor says, if you're being restricted over an extended period 'they better get you some auditions!' There are three options suggested by actors if you're in this situation. The first is to focus on doing the things that won't annoy even the most controlling agent (see pages 106–107). The second option is to present the problem. Ask for a meeting, explain yourself clearly and find agreement on some direct marketing you can do. The third (and perhaps riskier) option is to keep busy under the radar regardless!

For free resources to help you make the most of the expert advice in this chapter, visit www.actorscareerbible.com/freestuff

8
NETWORKING

Among actors I spoke to, the topic of networking was liable to induce groans and a fair bit of head-scratching. But networking effectively can be a lot simpler than you might imagine and industry interviewees offer plenty of tips on how to take the stress out of it.

Use the advice in this chapter to work on:

- Understanding the basics of networking
- Finding opportunities
- Using your network

What actually is networking?

I know I need to do more … but it gives me the most profound internal cringe.

Actor, five years out of drama school

Experienced actors explain that for actors, 'networking' is a broad term, covering:

1 Anything you do to strengthen your current industry relationships
2 Anything you do to create new industry relationships

'You don't have to sell, sell, sell,' explains one busy actor. Networking can be as easy as going about your normal daily acting life: bumping into people on a trip to the theatre or having an evening out with actor-friends. And every time you involve yourself in the industry in some way – going to a class, going for an audition or taking a job – you are strengthening or creating connections without having to try too hard. Interviewees advise you don't even think of this sort of thing as networking (with one actor saying it would be 'a bit creepy' if you did).

In fact, a highly successful performer advises taking a 'gently gently' approach to the whole concept whenever you can. Rather than aggressively pursuing new contacts in the hunt for a career boost, instead 'focus on *developing* relationships. All you need to do (when you meet people) is make a good impression. Then, once the relationship has reached some sort of maturity, help will come naturally, rather than you awkwardly forcing it.'

This view was echoed by agents and casting teams, who say they're more likely to warm to you if you don't see every new person as a chance to sell yourself. And time and time again, actors pointed out that the benefits of networking tend to reveal themselves over the long term, and in ways you won't necessarily expect: 'My current agent first approached me after a tip from a director who'd done a workshop with us years ago at drama school'; 'I got a radio job recently because I'd worked with the lead actress a while ago and she'd been asked for suggestions'; 'I was an unpaid extra but made an impression on the director ... two years later I was playing the lead in his first London show'.

Our 'gently gently' advocate highlights that 'it might be the second or third time you meet someone over a decade that suddenly something comes of it', and that a more relaxed approach is especially useful if you're new to the industry and finding your confidence with networking.

The networking basics

I try to do the simple things well; I've found those add up.

                                                                    Busy actor

To help you get started making connections in the industry, interviewees suggest some simple tips any actor can follow.

Make sure you're easy to search for online

Even if you don't yet have the confidence to reach out, make sure people have the chance to find you. Career coaches advise you start with Twitter so you're contactable and can post links to your CV and advertise your work. You can then investigate more involved options, including creating a website or managing an IMDb page (see Chapter 9 for more details).

Understand appropriate ways to make contact

A career-coach highlights, 'it can be quite hard, especially for young actors, to know where the boundaries are when interacting with (people from the industry)'. But learn to use the right contact methods for the right people and networking becomes much less fraught. The main rule to follow is that Facebook and Twitter are easy ways to stay linked to actors and directors you've worked with but agents and casting directors discourage actors from contacting them through social media, preferring an email or for an actor to go via an agent. Simple!

Stay on top of what's going on in the industry

Keeping tabs on what's going on in the industry – doing some research, seeing shows and finding ways to get involved – will broaden the number of people and projects you're genuinely excited to talk about; key for networking effectively. You'll also be more likely to pick up industry-references with people you chat to and recognize a name when you're introduced to someone new.

Know your crowd

Confident networkers advise you do a bit of homework on who's who and what's what before any sort of industry-related event. Being able to distinguish the cast from the casting director at someone else's wrap-party or press-night will oil the wheels of conversation and, perhaps more importantly, prevent you looking like you won a competition to be there. And if you're attending a convention or talk, knowing who the speakers are and a little bit about their work will make it that much easier to start conversations.

Practise talking about your work with confidence

Agents and casting directors emphasize how important it is that actors talk about themselves and their work in a positive way, avoiding any tone of apology about their career or negative responses like 'I'm not up to much really.' However, most performers interviewed agree this isn't always easy, especially if you've been out of work for a while.

To find a more positive tone, interviewees recommend first reminding yourself of previous successes, and re-finding interest in the things you have done, are doing and would like to do next. Second, if someone is asking about what you've been working on, actors suggest liberal use of the word 'Recently' in your answer. If in doubt you can even throw a 'Most' in there; 'Most recently I was working on ...' covers all bases.

The third common piece of advice here is you don't have to be talking about jobs to be talking about your career. Anything positive will do: a brilliant workshop, a great teacher you've been working with, a play you saw last week. After all, you never know what the person you're talking to will pick up on.

Finally, if someone is asking what you're doing next and you don't have a ready response, turn what you'd *like* to do next into a talking point: for example, 'Most recently I was working on a TV comedy and would like to do more of that'; or 'I'd really love to work with director X/ theatre company Y and have been seeing their shows.' You can even turn a current obstacle into a future challenge. Rather than complain, 'I haven't had a telly audition for two years,' say, 'I've been working mainly in theatre recently, but I'm focusing on getting more TV work.'

Keep a record of your contacts

'I wish I'd kept a list of casting directors who'd been to see my first show,' a former drama school student laments, one of many I spoke to who recommend maintaining a simple record of the various people you come across in the industry, or who come to see your work. You can do this easily with a spreadsheet or file on your computer – see Chapter 2 for more on this.

Opportunities for networking

Things will probably work out better than the scary version in your head.

Actor, three years of drama school

Many of the opportunities for networking listed here are simple and low stress, and therefore a great way to build confidence. Others require a little more boldness; you can work your way up to these or, as one career coach says, 'if you are able to get a "Fuck it!" attitude then you go full-tilt at everything.'

Make the most of your drama school or uni

Friendships and connections made during training can lead to benefits lasting well into an actor's professional live. 'The main source of support (once you're in the industry) comes from people in your year and surrounding years,' one graduate told me, with another detailing, 'I keep in touch with my drama school mates and let them know if I've read a script I think they'd be good for. This sort of thing organically creates a network of friends who watch each other's backs; and keeps their eyes peeled for parts that perhaps might suit you too.' A university graduate meanwhile described the bonus of studying alongside 'not just actors but writers, directors and producers you're connected to socially who may be able to hook you up'.

Others gave examples of the practical benefits of staying in contact with your drama school or uni ('the library continues to be a useful support'; 'they lent us rehearsal room space'). And many actors recommend staying in touch with staff and teachers, with a graduate saying, 'I occasionally ask their advice about parts I may be auditioning for or working on; their expertise is invaluable.' Others I spoke to had taken advantage of graduate classes and the chance to participate in readings and workshops. Some had found opportunities for non-acting work via their course staff, getting them through a period of unemployment. And there were even stories where staff had put graduates in contact with new agents and recommended them for jobs.

If you're still training, the advice therefore is to make contact with as many students, alumni and staff as possible, even if it's just a Facebook friendship request or a Twitter follow. Keep a record of who comes to see your final shows and showcases, and anyone from the industry who comes to talk to your year-group. Once you've left, check what's on offer to graduates, reconnect with people through social media and keep your drama school/uni updated with your details.

If your course offers mentorship schemes linking students to alumni, then actors say this is well worth making the most of. A graduate explains that mentors can 'soothe any worries or concerns' about entering the profession, with another highlighting 'they may bring people to your shows'. The benefits can extend further, with one actor revealing, 'my mentor got me a meeting with their agent', and another saying, 'they let me know that they were casting a play that I could potentially be in. I let my agent know, got an audition and after a couple of recalls, the part.'

Search for your own mentors

'If a drama school doesn't pair you with someone', a performer advises, 'write off to an actor and ask them. Many people have a sense of the acting industry as a community, and sometimes actors might suddenly have a bit of time on their hands to help you.' If you're on a course or have just graduated, their advice is to contact alumni; explain you're entering the industry and would welcome any advice they could offer. If you're already in the profession, then build these relationships with people you've worked with. Alternatively, contact a performer you admire but don't know yet; send them an email or a letter to where they're performing, asking for any advice or even a quick coffee. This might sound bold, but actors say that if you approach people with politeness and professionalism, then you can't go too far wrong.

Hang out more with your friends!

Actor-interviewees gave many instances where friends in the industry had supported them – from offering a shoulder to cry on to making recommendations that led to agents and jobs. For many, spending more time with the people they already know is the easiest way to expand their network. A recent graduate told me, 'I see as many plays as it is possible to, especially ones with friends in. All this can get your face seen by more people … you might meet the cast, and maybe the director.' The advice therefore is to take up opportunities to see your friends' shows and invite them to yours, go to industry events together or just use this as an excuse to spend more time with them in the pub – it all counts!

You're also encouraged to offer out help. 'Be a bit selfless because it will come back,' explains one performer, with others giving examples: 'I once helped a colleague on a film set put herself on tape for an audition. Months later I got a call out of the blue for a job based on her recommendation'; 'I helped some people making a short film by driving the lighting lorry and I met loads of people!'; 'I suggest people for short films and plays, or if I can't teach a class that week, I hook my friend up … they do the same for me.'

I spoke to several actors who had even set up regular meet-ups. These range from a gathering of friends reading a play with a glass of wine to groups that meet weekly taking it in turns to lead a class for each other. Actors say starting larger groups and hiring rooms takes a bit of organizing, but if you've got the will this is a good way to stay in touch.

Stay in touch with your more distant contacts

'Keep connections alive and firing!' urges one performer, with other actors agreeing that sending someone a little catch-up text, email or tweet every so often can be enough to keep your more tenuous relationships going. You can even rekindle an old connection with an update email on what you've been doing, a 'How are you?' or 'Do you fancy a coffee and a catch-up?' message over social media.

An actor with a number of years' experience explains the benefits: 'I do try to stay in touch with people, and it doesn't take much – I just send a quick email every so often. It means that once you have something to invite them to or you can help them in some way or you need their help, then you can make proper contact.'

Make the most of industry organizations

Organizations like Spotlight or Equity offer all sorts of great networking opportunities, including classes and professional development sessions. If you're like some of the actors I spoke to who admit they don't make the most of their memberships, check to see what you're missing out on; follow organizations on social media, explore their websites and make sure they've got your latest contact details.

Actors suggest lots of ways to get engaged in the industry, beyond what just lands in your lap. Organizations like the Actor's Centre, the Actors' Guild and weekend drama schools like the Unseen offer opportunities to go to classes, workshops and professional development talks, and as one actor describes 'meet like minds'. One proactive actor suggests looking out for workshops offered by theatre companies you're interested in. This is not only a way to learn and meet new people, but also a chance to get on the radar of companies you want to work for. Bookmark websites and sign up to email lists to make sure you get a place. Another good option, especially early in your career, is to audition for showcases run by groups like Triforce. The best ones have casting directors and agents on the panel, and you'll meet lots of new actors as well. Casting director workshops are another popular suggestion; the Actors Company LA offer these and were highly recommended by one performer.

You can find lists of these types of opportunities in the *Actors and Performers Yearbook* or use the advice on page 16 of this guide to search for your own.

Give your best to auditions and jobs

According to actors, casting directors and agents, turning up for auditions fully prepared and with a good attitude will mean you'll build relationships with the people in the room, regardless of whether or not you get the part. 'Casting directors and directors use the same people over and over again,' one performer explains. 'They know what kind of job they will do, they know that they are not any hassle, they know how they rehearse. With new people they are always taking a risk.'

Meanwhile, the networking benefits of working are considered so great that, while the odd high-level agent suggests actors should be picky at the beginning of their careers, most interviewees share the view of a successful performer who told me, 'graduates need to recognize that work breeds more work. Too often I see young actors turning things down in their first few years and missing an opportunity to start fruitful working relationships. I'm not saying do everything but be alive to the way the business works rather than riding your ego to the dole queue.'

Another successful, experienced performer takes this further, advising that, where you can, doing low/no pay jobs, workshops and readings will create important connections for you, especially at the beginning of your career: 'You always meet interesting people who you may work with one day. I once did a rehearsed reading at a theatre studio, was seen by a casting director and got a role in my first movie ... so that was cool.' Importantly, they add, 'I said "Yes" as long as I could afford to take the time off work.' And they warn, don't spread yourself too thin if you've already got something on the go: 'You don't want to compromise your other work.'

Once you're on a job, as one busy performer advises, 'always be on time; a good rule is to multiply the number of minutes you are late by the amount of people in the room you have kept waiting. Research, commit and be dedicated to your role, regardless of what you may think of the script or the job. Take direction well. And collaborate; you'll make much deeper and more complex work than any individual could.' Another actor echoes this, saying, 'without sucking up or fawning, being pleasant goes a long way to generating a reputation that will help you get jobs through recommendations. The parish is very small and word spreads fast.'

You can make the most of the networking opportunities available on jobs by following our busy performers' tips. One told me, 'I look up a little bit about the people I'm going to be working with. I can then pick their brains about cool projects they worked on and how they got where they got to. Sometimes, seeing my enthusiasm, they've even suggested I contact who they've worked with and drop their name.' Another explains that being on set is a great way to pick up casting gossip: 'Film and television is more tricky to find out about other than through an agent [but] once you're working it becomes easier to tune in to what's coming up. Production drivers and hair and make-up teams seem to be booked earliest for subsequent jobs, so they're useful to quiz about what they're going on to next.' This actor also highlights the value of putting yourself out there rather than waiting for things to come to you: 'I was acting at a theatre and the morning after we'd opened the show I went to introduce myself to the head of their project development department and I told them how much I'd love to help with workshopping new shows. I ended up getting to know lots of directors, writers and actors by doing this which led to future job opportunities.'

Produce your own projects

For a few actors interviewed, starting their own projects was part of fulfilling a long-held ambition. However, a side-benefit was meeting new contacts and performing in front of new people in the industry. This is a topic for a whole other book but one actor I spoke to who'd been there and done it offers some common advice: 'Take that first step. Don't think about all the other ones after that. When you've done that first one, then take another one, take another one, then – you've got it – another one!'

Build your confidence with face-to-face networking

A great way to build your confidence with networking is attending events like Surviving Actors and smaller talks or seminars run by theatres and industry organizations. As one actor explains, 'while it's natural to feel a bit awkward (when networking generally), everyone at these events is in the same boat'.

Less appealing for many actors is, as one outlines, 'getting dressed up to the nines going to press nights and parties and trying to talk to powerful people'. In fact, this is something many I spoke to actively avoid, with another performer describing it as 'the most difficult, ugly side of networking'.

Luckily, there are lots of tips out there. While one actor acknowledges, 'it's a bit like cold-calling, you have to be prepared for some pain and discomfort', they add reassuringly, 'if you do it in the right way, with professionalism, dignity and a lack of negativity it will only help'. Most people agree that once you boil it down it's fairly simple and that the risks to your career are fairly small! 'Everyone is just a person; a good thing to remember,' says one experienced TV actor. Their advice is, 'don't go over the top. Have a little chat, keep it short, sweet, say something funny or just be kind and nice.' A top agent meanwhile advises thinking of networking simply as 'listening to people and having a positive, friendly tone', while an experienced actor notes, 'most people know the score and will be comfortable enough with you starting a conversation'. A confident actor perhaps puts it most plainly: 'If you go up to a stranger at a party and politely introduce yourself, as long as you don't do anything weird, the likelihood is someone will talk to you for a couple of minutes.'

With this in mind it's easier to take on the advice of another performer: 'You can get in to that "I want to stay at home vs go to things" problem … But you should just go! You never know who you might meet!' However, as one producer highlights, 'you can't force yourself to (talk to people). It won't work, you won't be relaxed.' The advice is that having a strategy can help here. For example, if you're worried about being ignored then focus on getting introductions via people you know. Or if you're feeling anxious about people thinking you're too pushy, limit how much you talk about yourself or the industry. Another option is to give yourself a time limit. An actor told me they'd been invited to their agent's big end-of-year party despite not knowing anyone. Giving themselves a strict time to leave and an event to go to afterwards made for an easier exit if they started to feel uncomfortable.

Once you're actually at an event, the advice is to drop any agenda. 'Never be obviously ambitious,' warns one actor, adding knowingly, 'they can smell it a mile off'. Instead, they say make your goal simply 'to have a good time'. This takes the pressure off; plus, you'll seem more approachable.

Successful actors also emphasize that you talk to anyone; networking isn't necessarily about boldly striding up to the most important or popular person in the room. Everyone at an event will be there for a good reason, and you can't be sure who'll be able to help you one day or who you'll bump into again. And as one experienced actor points out, remember that 'everyone you talk to will have their own network of people'. So, in effect, by chatting to one person, you're potentially connecting to all the people they know.

The advice on approaching people is fairly straightforward. If you see someone you dream of working with then follow the be-polite-and-professional rule. As one actor says, 'there's nothing wrong with going up to people, telling them you love their work and having a quick two minute conversation. If you're worried about interrupting, catch them really quickly just as they're leaving: "Sorry to disturb you, I love your work …"'. If you are going to an event with friends, help each other out, introducing one another to people you each know. One actor told

me, 'I was at a posh awards-do with a producer and was able to introduce him to people as a way in because they recognized the work
he'd done.' Other people had less glamorous but equally encouraging
examples. If you are going to an event alone the advice is start by talking to anybody you vaguely recognize, then introduce yourself to any
friends in their group. If you don't recognize anyone then the easiest
option is to keep visible; stay by the bar and wait for people to talk to
you (just don't get too drunk). If you're feeling braver then your best bet
is to find someone else who's on their own and introduce yourself.

Key to successful face-to-face networking is to drop your pride.
Several of the actors I spoke to have an awkward story where they'd
been ignored, brushed off or been called the wrong name at an industry
event. Do what they do and try not to take it personally; if you follow
the advice in this chapter and someone is still rude then that's probably
more to do with them than you. And if you're re-introducing yourself,
one actor advises, 'don't be afraid to remind people, but to avoid awk-
wardness do it with the possibility they won't remember you: "I met
you" rather than "You met me" ... "It was X amount of years ago" ... "I'd
just come out of drama school" etc.'

Once you're chatting, there's a key piece of advice that comes
up again and again: 'If the conversation turns to the industry, aim to
find out about the person you are talking to'; 'Listen and find out their
story: why they're there, what they do, have been doing, are doing
next'; 'Recognize other peoples' priorities and respond to them.' When
the time comes to talk about yourself, remember the number one rule is
to be positive! 'Talk about the people you've worked with; there may be
a connection,' says one performer, while another says encouragingly,
'people feed off enthusiasm and passion so always have something to
come to the party with ... tell your fabulous story!'

If a conversation is drawing to an end, the advice from an experienced performer is to only 'ask for people's numbers or details if it
is a natural next move from what you have been talking about', adding, 'higher status people especially may be unwilling to give out personal info to people they have just met'. If you're unsure, one actor
says you're better off 'cutting the conversation. If people pick up you
have an ulterior motive and you push through, at worst you'll alienate
someone. And at best you will get a result but someone who eventually gets your email and thinks "Oh shit, it's them"'. If it doesn't feel

right to ask for someone's details, actors commonly advise following the person on Twitter after the event or, as an experienced performer suggests, 'just send a follow-up ("Nice to meet you") email the next day'. Alternatively, take this even simpler approach described by another performer: 'Make a good impression and then leave it, because you will probably see them again.'

Using your network

It's a people-based industry.

Career coach

As explained already in this chapter, many of the benefits of networking will come to you automatically. The more you consolidate and expand your network the more likely these pleasant surprises will arise. Beyond that, using your network is all about maintaining a balance between keeping relationships going and asking for help when you need it. If you get to a point where you want to ask for something but can't find the confidence, then one of the most well-connected actors interviewed suggests thinking of your request not as a burden on the other person but 'an offer', explaining 'people often actually like the chance to help'.

If you are looking for help don't limit your search to your own contacts. Remember, you are also potentially connected to everyone they know so ask for introductions and recommendations. As one of our more experienced networkers advises, 'any sort of relationship can be used as a start; you just need a point of connection. So, if you want to contact a particular director make your friend who's worked with them several times that point of connection. As long as you don't think it would be inappropriate, if someone knows someone that can help you, ask them to put you in touch.'

Use the other chapters in this part of the book to help you act on the information you get from your friends and contacts: follow-up on casting gossip and take up offers to recommend you to agents and casting directors. And if people do help you, follow the advice of this busy networker: 'Make sure you nurture that relationship once the door has been opened: give them gratitude and help them back when you can.'

For free resources to help you make the most of the expert advice in this chapter, visit www.actorscareerbible.com/freestuff

9
ONLINE MARKETING

This chapter covers advice on how to promote yourself using a personal website, the IMDb (Internet Movie Database) website, Twitter and other social media. You'll find tips from performers who have built up big online followings, as well as guidelines from casting teams and agents on how to make a good impression.

Use the advice in this chapter to work on:

- Finding the right options for you

- Building your online presence

- Using online marketing for research and finding opportunities

---

Personal websites

I don't know how much of a difference it's made, but I think it can make you look professional ... and one day hopefully it will be good for America.

Actor (with ambitions abroad), three years into the profession

Opinion was split among interviewees on whether or not actors need a website. For instance, while one director-producer described them as 'the most essential thing!', the next casting director I spoke to frowned at the idea performers make them a priority. What the range of reactions suggests is that, unlike in America, websites aren't mandatory for

British performers, confirmed by the many actors I spoke to that get by without one.

For actors who are new to the profession and on a budget, the advice is to focus on bigger priorities first, for example paying for marketing materials and casting sites. If you're in a position where you've got those sorted and have the money to spend, increasing your internet presence becomes a valid next aim. While casting directors and agents generally use Spotlight to find and research actors, as one West End producer reveals, they also 'look up actors they're going to call in, putting a name into Google and hitting the return key'. The question then is, is building a website the most effective way for you to increase your visibility online?

The first thing to do is google your name to check what already appears. As one experienced actor suggests, 'your agent's site or IMDb profile are good references', and spending money on a website may not be necessary if either of these pop up at the top of your search. If you're not happy with the search results, investing in an IMDb subscription is recommended as a better choice for actors with decent TV and film credits. But if you haven't yet made many appearances onscreen, a professional-looking website is considered a better option.

Creating a website

'If you present (industry figures) with something that looks lazy, they'll think you are a lazy person,' a career coach emphasizes. Luckily, they add that achieving something professional 'is really simple'.

Companies like Squarespace, Wix and Wordpress help you build low-maintenance sites without spending crazy amounts. In terms of effort, one performer told me, 'initially creating it takes a little time; after that it's just chunks every so often to add new photos [for example]'. There are trial periods and discount codes available (e.g. lots of podcasts are sponsored by website builders and offer money off).

You can opt for 'a basic thing', as one actor prefers, 'just so there is something there; a homepage with a photo and a link to your Spotlight, a contact email for yourself or your agent'. Other actors interviewed added extra pages for an about/bio section, CV, photo gallery, showreel, latest news, contact details including links to social media and quotes from reviews.

IMDb (Internet Movie Database)

IMDb will sell the idea that you are higher-level, working actor.
Performer with a wide range of US and UK screen credits

The IMDb website is a database of screen projects and all the people involved in making them. For us British-based performers the site has two main benefits: increasing online presence and researching the industry.

There are two versions of the site. The free-to-access IMDb allows you to do basic research; you can find out what screen-casting teams have worked on and have coming up, and as one actor explains, 'you can research meetings and follow actor's career paths'. You can also view your page (if you have any professional screen credits or you've appeared in any project that has been listed on the site, then the people at IMDb will create a profile for you).

IMDb Pro is the subscription version of the site. At the time of writing, the annual cost is over £100, and the big question is, is it worth signing up for? If you don't have the budget then the easy answer is 'No'. Casting directors and agents say that IMDb Pro is not absolutely vital to your career, especially if you're at an early stage, and there are bigger priorities to spend your money on first. However, if you've got your main priorities sorted (and assuming you have the budget) interviewees suggest three main reasons to pay for IMDb Pro.

The first is to refine your internet presence. By signing up to IMDb Pro you can create an impressive online profile that will appear near the top of internet searches. Therefore, IMDb Pro is often recommended as a better investment than a website for actors who have good screen credits. If you don't have many screen credits, a website may be a better choice; you'll be able to get more information on there and produce something more impactful.

A second good reason for considering IMDb Pro is if you're searching for a new representation or casting teams to target, and you're struggling to narrow the field or find contact details. By signing up, you can access email addresses for casting directors, agents (and lists of any of their clients that have a page on the site), as well as directors, producers and many others.

Finally, some actors use IMDb Pro to work towards longer-term career aims. A busy and experienced performer explains, 'In America, IMDB is gospel and will have a big effect on how they see you.' For most actors at the start of their careers the US isn't yet a consideration, but if you're at a stage where your career is developing, signing up will help you take advantage of opportunities later down the line.

The cost of subscription is understandably off-putting for many actors, so if you still find yourself um-ing and ah-ing, check how other actors with similar experience to you use the site (do they have a developed IMDb profile?), learn more by sneaking a look via any friends with a subscription and take advantage of the 30-day trial period.

Setting up your IMDb Pro page

The site does a lot of the work for you, listing your screen appearances and agent details. Check that all of these are correct, especially the 'Known For' section, which displays your most impressive credits.

Big celebs have IMDb bios that read like a cross between a Wikipedia entry and a fan page. However, for most actors any existing bio will be very basic. The advice is to tweak what's there so it's as impressive as possible while keeping it short. Write in the third person ('X is an actor …') and highlight your best credits ('… who has appeared in Y and Z'). You can also mention your training and if you've been nominated or won any awards. Any more than that at early career stages and you'll increase the chances of it looking like you've edited it yourself (not the intended effect). You can get a better gauge on what's appropriate at various career levels by searching through performers' profiles.

Upload your showreel (if you have one) to IMDb, as well as a range of photos; this is the place to put any mid- or full-length body shots, publicity photos, screen shots or professional snaps of you at industry parties. As one (admittedly very successful) actor says, 'make sure you have lots of photos on there, red carpet especially. Get them off Google. If they've got the copyright name across them then contact the photographer and sweet them up a bit: "I really like the photo. Do you mind if

I take this? I'll obviously copyright you" … they will either give it to you for free or a little bit of money.'

Your main photo should identifiably be you, and if you can, choose from a mid-/full-length photo, publicity shot or photo of you at an industry event. If you don't yet have any of these options (this will be the case for most actors starting out) then use a colour headshot; your most glossy one will probably work best. Don't put up a range of headshots on the site; you'll kill the illusion of success!

Social media

I hate it … but I know I need to do more.

Actor, five years in the profession

Effective social media, one savvy actor explains, 'is about repetition; giving your name a chance to appear every so often on industry and audience feeds. You follow a casting director … then later send a Tweet about a play they've worked on … a few months on you're tagged in a photo of an actor they know on Instagram … two months on from that you're promoting your show, one of your mutual followers retweets it, and they see it. The same thing happens with information coming to you: You follow a theatre on Instagram, Facebook and Twitter and you start to get a picture of which actors work there, the casting directors, workshops and open auditions.'

Of course, not every actor I spoke to was happy promoting themselves online. As a reluctant tweeter explains, 'the demands of this career can take you to places where you feel uncomfortable, and the need to sell yourself doesn't always fit well with people who just want to be actors.' A simple way 'to limit the cringe factor', as one actor puts it, is to have some sort of presence but not necessarily engage day to day. 'Set things up and then every so often just have a quick tidy-up and a quiet tweak', recommends one performer; you'll still get some of the benefits but won't feel like you're being pushy. Another actor-interviewee suggests, 'use genuine-ness to avoid feeling icky', with another performer explaining, 'there's a big difference between expressing something that comes from you and doing things to control how you want to be perceived'. You can achieve this by primarily promoting yourself when you are doing something industry related, as opposed to during quiet periods when it can, as one actor describes, 'feel like you're begging for a job'.

Alternatively, of course, you can just bite the bullet. 'You may have to abandon your principles and embrace the hashtag,' says an experienced actor, while another says, 'marketing online can feel a little bit rigid, like you are not being yourself, but if you want to be yourself then you are in the wrong industry. Early on you need it; [later in your career] you can reject those self-promotion things if you don't like them.'

Whatever approach you decide on, patience at early career stages is key. As one experienced actor explains, 'it can be distracting and upsetting if you don't get many likes … but over time you will begin to build support and interest'.

Twitter

Twitter is ideal, a career coach explains, 'if anyone in the industry wants to make a connection with you, message you or get your details'. They add, 'you can keep all your relationship bubbling along through likes, tweets and messages' and that all this 'connection building', as they put it, looks good from the outside: 'Casting directors will see that you're contactable and you're engaged.' Twitter also gives you the chance to advertise your marketing materials and jobs to the industry and begin building an audience for your work.

As well as all that, an experienced screen performer emphasizes, you get 'an absolute ton of information at your fingertips'. A lot of this will come to you via other peoples' feeds but as they explain, 'there's so much information you can find yourself. Search hashtags for anything you're interested in like #showreel or #actingclass, have a scroll through and you might find something useful. Or throw a question out there – "I'm looking for some new photos, any recommendations?" Depending on the followers you've got you might get suggestions or retweets and then somebody contacting you.' You can even find jobs, with a London fringe theatre director one of several who told me, 'I posted castings for my last show on Twitter.'

If you have some doubts but still want to benefit, then actors say a basic level of engagement is easy to maintain. 'Twitter is a way of indirectly engaging with the industry', an actor interviewed observes, one of several who recommends a gentle approach. Follow theatres, casting directors and production companies; pick up information and over time slowly build up connections; check it every so often and send out the odd retweet. You then have the account there if you need it for research, contacting someone or promoting your work.

Setting up your Twitter account

To create your handle, interviewees recommend choosing something as close to your acting name as possible. This will make it easier for industry figures and audiences to recognize and find you online. For your photo, you can use a colour headshot but if you want it to be slightly less actory then, as an experienced Twitter user suggests, 'you can put up any nice photo of you'.

Some bios are all business, announcing that the person is an actor, listing work and linking to an agent site or Spotlight page. Others are much more informal, a quirky quip. 'A mixture of the two works well,' says one career coach. 'It shows some personality, but means you are contactable and markets you as an actor.'

Include a link in the bio itself and/or separately below. There are a few options: an agent's version of your CV, your Spotlight page, your website, your IMDb page, a link to any current/upcoming work you're doing, a link to your showreel if it's hosted on a site like Vimeo or a link to your Instagram. Pick out what's going to show you at your best and keep your profile uncluttered; one or two is normally fine.

Who to follow

Twitter is an easy way to consolidate new relationships without being too forward. As a career coach suggests, if you meet new industry-people out and about, 'rather than hand someone a business card, you can follow them on Twitter the next day'.

Following casting directors, producers, directors, writers, production companies and agents will help you decide if they are realistically worth targeting for work, given your previous credits and other selling points. You'll pick up information on how they prefer to be contacted and what they expect at auditions or meetings. And you'll also find opportunities to attend workshops, talks and possibly even castings. If you're unsure where to start, or find yourself getting overwhelmed, the advice from one actor is simply to 'follow a theatre because you've worked there, or because you might want to work there in the future', or, in other words, focus on your most realistic opportunities *and* where you want to head to next. Those feeds will throw up lots of new, similar names, and Twitter will suggest new, similar accounts for you to follow. Following other actors meanwhile will give you access to lots of extra information, plus you'll learn more about what to tweet; and who knows, you might make a new friend.

Experienced actors advise making the most of Twitter lists to categorize and streamline information. You can do this in a general way, for example grouping together theatres or industry news feeds. But lists are really useful for working towards specific career goals. For example, if you're currently targeting a particular area of the industry, then create a list of casting directors who work in that area; if you're looking for new representation, group together your top agent choices; and if you're looking for a photographer or showreel editor then create lists so you don't miss tweets about their latest work and discounts. To create a list, go to the List tab, come up with a name and start adding feeds (you don't have to be following a feed to add it to your list). As one actor warns, 'anyone you add to a public list will be notified', so you're advised to make the majority of your industry-related lists private, especially when adding casting teams and agents. If you do want to make a list public carefully choose the title and who you add. You can also look at others' lists for further ideas on who to follow.

Easy tweets for actors

'People want to see a bit of personality, a little part of you. If they want just the actor-stuff then they'll look you up on Spotlight,' says one popular Twitter user. 'I tweet a mixture of acting stuff and stupid things I've seen, like a funny sign or a photo or an article that makes me laugh. Then if casting directors look at your feed, it's sort of a mini-introduction before they've met you. And if you're your funny interesting self and don't take it too seriously, you'll probably end up with more followers.'

If you're struggling to find 'acting stuff' to tweet, there is plenty of advice. If you're on a job, promote it using a pinned tweet and/or put a link to the show in your bio. Following associated feeds will give you opportunities for retweets and quoted tweets. Your own photos, videos and comments are all good (as long as you're careful you're not breaching copyright or revealing on-set secrets!). And tagging the show, people involved, company and using hashtags will, in the words of one actor, help you 'capture some of the audience'. As another actor suggests, you can do this all quite informally and gently: 'The odd time of saying "Hey look, I'm on the telly" and people slowly but surely cotton on.'

If you're not currently working, then there are still lots of opportunities for acting-related tweets. A career coach I spoke to advises getting involved in the industry, and 'using Twitter to say "Thanks!"' If you've been to a press night, industry party, workshop, class or seminar, thank the people involved for inviting you or passing on great info or advice. Reply to and thank audience members that comment on your shows. And thank headshot photographers, showreel editors or anyone else that helps you. Another common suggestion is to post mini-reviews. One experienced actor explains, 'if you like something, recommend it and tag the theatre. For their PR, theatres look out for actors and they may retweet you. Then the people that follow those theatres will see that: "Ooo I know that guy" or "They're interesting" … "I'll follow."' The same advice applies for films, TV shows, web series, scripts, books, blogs – anything industry related you want to recommend.

And if you're really lacking inspiration, just retweeting other people and organizations is an easy way to keep your feed going, feel like you've done something and who knows, it may get you on someone's radar.

Twitter etiquette for actors

Perhaps the most common 'definitely don't!' when using social media is directly contacting casting teams and agents that you don't have a pre-existing relationship with, with one casting director describing it as 'a disastrous strategy … it's too intrusive'. In fact, expect industry figures to be very selective about how they interact with actors. Unless you're friends, have a previous close working relationship or you have a level of profile that is attractive to them, you're unlikely to get followed back (and definitely don't contact them asking them to follow you!). An experienced Twitter user explains, 'by all means occasionally like, retweet and respond. You can be funny or matter of fact, and there's no harm in going, "I saw that the other night, thought it was amazing." But if you start getting too heavy – weekly CV tweeting, "Here's my new headshot" – that's just going to seem creepy. And don't constantly ask them questions – "I really liked this but what did you think?" – cos you're basically saying, "interact with me". Consider Twitter like talking to someone on a bus having never met them; if you're too full-on, or come across as being too needy or intense, people are going to be put off.'

Actor-interviewees say social media isn't the place to vent your industry frustrations ('Keep it positive!'), divulge negative personal issues ('I rarely discuss my personal life on social media') or criticize other people's work ('Don't be insulting!'). And while you're encouraged to be yourself, one performer cautions: 'you have to be a bit wary about what you're saying. Big producers and casting directors will check peoples' social media and if you start making slightly dodgy jokes and things like that they could be like "That's probably not the person for this project." '

Facebook

'Predominantly my Facebook is personal, for friends and family; my public profiles are Twitter and Instagram.' This is the approach of one successful actor I spoke to, shared by the vast majority of other actors interviewed. Industry figures back this up, with one casting director saying, 'it's fine if I've met someone and they want to friend me, but it's got to be someone I've got a connection to, not just a random, someone I've never met and never heard of'.

While Facebook isn't recommended for aggressive self-promotion, you can use it for staying in touch with industry people you've met, advertising jobs you're working on, asking for advice and researching certain aspects of the industry. And several actors say Facebook groups can be invaluable. One I spoke to advises other female performers to 'become a member of BOSSY. It's great for everything theatre related'.

Instagram

Instagram is another way to connect and be seen, offers further opportunities for following organizations and industry figures, and provides extra material for your Twitter feed. An actor and career coach explains you can 'populate your own myth', creating the idea that you are busy, confident, happy and successful (or at least heading that way). Of course, you can include anything you want but photos on set, in rehearsal, at workshops, at the theatre, out and about with other actors are all useful for marketing yourself (though our career coach advises that, if you're ever unsure, 'check any contracts to see what you can and can't put online').

Connecting everything up

You have to put things out there, throw the net wide and see what happens.

Successful screen and stage actor

Opting to have photos and comments appear across Twitter, Instagram and Facebook will create more tweets and posts for you, and – along with links – will hopefully draw followers from one account to the other. If you want to be extra-strategic with social media then consider services like Crowdfire. These can come with a cost, but some actor-interviewees had used them to generate followers. Another common tips is to concentrate your posts on Instagram and Twitter focused on particular areas. As one actor explains, if your followers see only 'five topics, that creates a brand in itself'.

For free resources to help you make the most of the expert advice in this chapter, visit www.actorscareerbible.com/freestuff

PART THREE
AUDITIONING

10
PREPARING FOR AUDITIONS

Many of the interviewees for this guide picked out preparing for auditions as the most important area an actor can try to improve on, with one leading agent emphasizing, 'you've got to do every meeting to the best of your ability. Don't turn up with a shitty product; make sure it's fucking good!' Meanwhile, an experienced actor admits (less swearily), 'I went to a lot of auditions underprepared and nervous in my first couple of years out. If I could go back, I'd be much less casual about everything; I'd turn up knowing it inside out.' This chapter will take you through all the advice.

Use the advice in this chapter to work on:

- Prioritizing what to prepare
- Improving each element of how you prepare

Prioritizing your prep

Every casting director will say, 'You have to be really prepared for an audition'. But what does that actually mean?

Actor, more than ten years in the profession

Before diving in to preparing for a meeting, take a few minutes to plan what you'll focus on. As one career coach outlines, it's useful to 'identify the competitive criteria that the audition will be decided on'. For example, if you're auditioning for a two-page TV scene that films in a couple of days' time, your focus might be on learning the lines, showing the casting team you're ready to shoot; for a regular role in a series set in the American South, you might prioritize nailing the accent; and for a play with a dense subject matter you might put a large part of your focus on background research. You can then balance this with doing the things that make you feel most relaxed. For example, for some actors I spoke to, not being 100 per cent on the lines makes them very nervous, so they commit lots of prep time to it; some like to read the script over and over, so they know the story inside out; while others say they don't feel their best unless they've dry-run the audition with a coach a few times.

Areas of preparation

There's nothing special that anyone else is doing that gives them a huge advantage over you.

Veteran casting director

As the quote above suggests, good preparation comes down to working hard on various simple tasks, and interviewees have plenty of advice on how you can do just that.

Reading the script

Casting teams generally expect you to read the entirety of scripts you're sent, and in almost all cases this will be a benefit to you. As one performer points out, 'you'll have thoughts about the entire project, and you'll show you've spent quality time with the script and value their production'. To give yourself the best chance, the advice is to have the script in some form with you at all times for reading on the go, and as one graduate says, 'drink a coffee … and put everything else back!'

Of course, as another actor highlights, sometimes 'it may be impossible' to get everything read in the short amount of time given, especially if you're sent several episodes of something. If you recognize that you're not going to be done in time, 'the key thing', as one performer explains, 'is to understand the story and who your character is in relation to that story'. One actor suggests, 'read a synopsis if you can find one', while another advises, 'focus on your scenes first, then the scenes where your character appears or is mentioned and maybe then your particular bit [your episode, act or section]. Skim-read or leave everything else for now.' In the room itself, admitting you haven't read it and then making excuses 'will annoy everyone involved and they'll not want you back', one actor explains. To avoid lying, a savvy graduate advises, 'just give an answer like "I thought it was great."' Assuming you're familiar with the script as a whole and have closely read your scenes, you'll still be able to discuss the story and the character capably enough.

Picking material

If you're asked to select material, an experienced casting director says simply, 'choose obvious scenes!', with other interviewees offering some tips to clarify: start with any scenes that your character is a major part of; contrasting scenes show the casting panel you can play different aspects of the character; picking a scene from the beginning of a script and one at the end can demonstrate your ability to play the character's full story-arc; any scene you have a strong connection to or particular interest in is a good choice.

If you're asked for a monologue or song, advice comes from one successful actor who says, 'choose something you love and feel great doing, which also shows your strengths. Always have a contrasting back-up. And remember who your core audience would be in the actual production; don't choose a Sarah Kane role for an audition piece if it's a company aimed at young children!'

Whatever you choose, a casting director says have your reason ready: 'If asked saying, "I thought these scenes were the best choices because X, Y and Z" ... well, now you've really got my attention.'

Research

Interviewees suggest four areas you can research in preparation for an audition. The sources listed on page 16 will help you with each of these.

First, you can research an aspect of the character or story. How much you do here will depend on what you need to feel prepared and the time available. As one actor says, 'for some auditions I might have a two minute look on Wikipedia … but (for others) I might read a whole book'.

A second research area is the casting team and the work they do. A career coach says 'pick out links: "I've just done X and I know you worked with actor Y."' A busy actor meanwhile advises: 'look for reasons why you're in the room: "Oh she cast that, which featured those three actors I worked with, that's where she's come across me."' This actor also recommends searching for information about a director's working style: 'Read up on them in interviews; not so you can quote it back to them, but so you can get their angle.'

Third, you can search for further information on the project itself. For instance, look up who else is involved beyond the people you're meeting, early plans for creative elements of the production and further details about the venue/s or dates. One actor highlights that this means you'll be more able to 'show a genuine interest and excitement'.

Finally, interviewees recommend researching the style of the play, show or film you're auditioning for. As one TV casting director explains, 'every piece of television [for example] is done differently. If it's a comedy, you have to find the *right type* of comedy.' For some projects, this can be a vital aspect of an actor's prep: for example, if you're auditioning for a TV series that is already on air or a theatre company where they expect you to have a passion for the work; as one casting director reveals, in these cases, 'it's an immediate turn-off if you say "I've never seen it."' They add that by researching the style of the project you'll also be better placed to 'contribute to any discussions in the room'.

If you are auditioning for an existing TV series it's recommended you catch an episode; casting directors say even watching a few minutes can help. Look on catch-up TV, for clips on YouTube or if you can't find it and can afford it, pay for a download or DVD. If you're auditioning for something brand new, then watching something in a similar genre may be of help (sometimes existing work is given as examples on casting briefs). The same advice applies to films that are part of a series or being directed or produced by people with a particular working style; get a sense of their work or general work in a similar style. For plays, if you have the time and money and there is something you can catch it can be worth the effort. If a project is based on source material, actors recommend referring to it if you have a few spare prep-hours. Less time-intensive options suggested by actors include searching for interviews with the writer, producer or director to get a sense of their preferred performance style/s or reading any previous reviews you can find.

While this is all useful advice, several performers warn of overdoing research: 'You can give yourself too much information that you don't need!'; 'Don't use it to procrastinate. The bulk of your time should be spent with the text'; 'Watch for it throwing your head: "They did all that!? Shit!"'. To help, an experienced actor suggests, 'Use research as an entry point to prep. Spend ten minutes looking up the casting team and then crack on. You can always come back to it if you have the time'. Another meanwhile warns: 'Don't do it minutes before you go in and panic because you find out they are massive.' If you haven't had time to research, '[wait till after the audition] as a point of closure and a reference for next time'.

However much you decide to do, most actors and casting directors agree with an actor who says 'wear the results of your research very lightly'. Another busy graduate explains, 'the mistake is to do it with the aim of impressing (the casting team); you're not doing it so you can casually drop it in the room'. Instead, they say 'it's about helping yourself, making yourself feel more confident'. A casting director I spoke to usefully describes this as 'an if-it-comes-up policy', with a very successful performer clarifying: 'if you do get those two minutes of chat then you can slot it in: "I saw X. Loved it. That scene with Y and Z." You're being authentic and you won't sound sucky-uppy.' Research will also throw up questions for you to ask; again the advice is these should be genuine, rather than an attempt to impress.

Actors underline that of course everything can change once you're in the room: 'Remember that your presumptions about a job will probably be inaccurate'; 'Know who you are going to be meeting. Then be prepared for it to change completely from the actual people'; 'Research directors to see if you've seen any of their work. Then forget about it. The impression you have built up in your head will almost always be completely wrong.'

Finally, meetings that involve some sort of discussion with the casting team may also cover your previous work. Actors interviewed say it's worth having a think or a look back over your CV so you're not left hesitating and fumbling.

Preparing an accent

'If there is an accent, you must do it. If you're unsure, check' is the simple advice of one experienced auditionee. Be aware that once you're in the meeting room you may also be asked to read the scenes in your own accent. Go to pages 4–5 for more advice.

Learning lines for screen projects

Whenever you can, the advice is to be off-book for a screen audition. However, if you're facing a Herculean line-learning task, a top agent reassures, 'don't worry, the casting director will know there's lots to do and they've only given you the meeting the night before.'

To give yourself the best chance, a busy TV figure says, 'you have to be prepared to work very fast and intensely the days before the audition,' with others saying they're constantly juggling their social and work commitments when meetings come in. As well as being flexible, take the script with you wherever you go and try free apps like Line Learner.

If you recognize you're going to struggle, don't stress yourself out by heroically pushing on; as one calm actor imparts, 'you want to limit, as far as possible, distracting thoughts and anxiety when you walk into the casting room'. Remember that learning the lines is not the object of the exercise, giving a good performance is, and plenty of actors I spoke to had got recalls and roles with a script in hand. A top agent says in this situation simply, 'aim to be off-book for at least one of the scenes and try to be familiar with the rest of the material'. A TV casting director says, once you're in the room, 'don't make excuses like, "I didn't have time to learn it." Just do the scenes as best as you can'. Another says encouragingly you're better off looking down at a script occasionally: 'Half-knowing it probably won't help. It may be better to read it; it will create a smoother performance. Take an all or nothing approach and commit to your choice!'

Learning lines for theatre auditions

'There is much less expectation for you to learn the lines so I like to let myself just be very familiar with the play and part,' says one actor-interviewee, offering common advice on theatre auditions. 'Very familiar' means, as another performer explains, 'you're still able to look up at who you're acting with every few moments.' In fact, as one director says, 'the less "on-book" you are, the more likely you'll be able to give a decent performance', and they advise practising with the script in hand and as far as possible learning sections where checking the script will break your flow (very quick dialogue or emotional speeches, for example). They add that if you've been given a short monologue or very short scenes to prepare with plenty of time, being off or nearly-off book will help your cause.

Making choices: preparing for performance and direction

Casting teams are consistent in what they say they want to see at auditions. A producer told me, 'essentially you want people to walk in having thought about the role and made a decision about it'; a director revealed 'bold choices are great, even if they are wrong … the worst thing for us to think about your audition is "Well, that was pretty forgettable, wasn't it"'; and a casting director said 'we almost always want you to offer something rather than go in asking, "Please tell me how to do it"'.

Experienced, successful actors agree: 'there isn't a "correct" way to do the role'; 'in an audition you shouldn't feel like you're intruding … you have every right to be there, and your version is your ticket'; 'come into the room with a truthful, committed and nuanced performance that will blow them away!'

While one actor says, 'don't be afraid to be left-field', another actor explains, you don't necessarily have to make crazy, whacky choices, just clear ones: 'You have to offer something. It could be a character choice, it could be a particular interpretation on the scene or it could just be pure naturalism.'

The problem, however, as one experienced actor explains, is 'if you prepare too heavily with your version of the character. Then [when you get direction] you'll be thrown.' Another performer outlines, 'the solution is to go in with an angle and another version and be expecting re-direction.' Make choices you're happy to walk in the room with and prepare or think about other feasible ways of playing the part, including how your performance would change were major circumstances in the brief or stage direction completely different. All this advice applies to recalls as well; keep an open mind, even if you've had success with your previous choices. One actor going up for a big movie explains, 'I did the first audition one way; did it exactly as the casting director had imagined. But then at the callback the director wanted it completely different.'

Beyond using what you find in the script, make choices and explore alternate possibilities by gleaning any information you can from the brief (see below), your agent if you're represented and any further research you do on the performance style of the piece. And while many actors I spoke to work by themselves to make their acting choices, some contact a coach to help and run the scenes a few times.

The brief (or breakdown) is a summary of the project, story and character that often gets sent out with a script (if you don't receive one check with your agent or, if you're not represented or going through them, the casting director). A casting director explains, 'you don't have to take [the brief] completely literally. Treat it as a guide only, to check you are not miles away or have misunderstood something. Take the essence of what they're saying, then read the script and get on with it.' If there are elements of the brief you're really unsure about, they advise 'ask your agent to ring up if in doubt ... "Do they want that or is it open?"' They finish by reminding actors 'that in the room things may turn out to be flexible, including basic physical things like hair colour or height or even accents. We might put a description, but for smaller roles especially, it won't always matter.'

If you're not sure which way to go with your choices, experienced actors advise prepping, then waiting for direction or clues once you're in the room. However, as this successful screen actor explains, sometimes 'you may have to take a leap into the dark. It may go wrong and be a bit embarrassing, they might see that you're not right for the part ... you should just show that you are a good actor and get on with your performance.'

Physical action and props

Casting teams and seasoned actors say to ignore props and stage direction unless they're absolutely vital for the scene. If there's some physical action that you feel is absolutely necessary, you can subtly suggest it: for example, taking a step forward for an important entrance.

Preparing for the casting room, camera and reading with casting directors

Use part of your prep-time to place people and objects you refer to, characters you speak to besides who you're reading with and the direction of any exits or entrances. For screen auditions, the advice is to do this making sure your eyeline stays as close to the edge of camera as possible.

Actors say you can also prepare for the various scenarios you might be presented with in the audition room. For example, think about or rehearse your scene: sitting down, standing up, walking round the room; a wider shot or close up, above your eyeline or below; imagining yourself in a small audition room or a huge hall, with your reading partner close to you or far away, or with a casting director either giving it everything, speaking incredibly quietly or distracted fiddling with the camera.

Your look and what to wear

The first and most obvious rule here is if the casting team asks you to wear something specific, wear it! The second, as one experienced performer emphasizes, is 'don't wear costume'. A casting director explains, 'you can look a little try-hard and gimmicky', with an agent saying more bluntly, 'you'll look weird'. Third, as one actor says, 'don't dress *against* the part'. An agent explains, 'be sensible; if you are going in for a lawyer don't turn up in shorts and a vest. If it's a period drama, don't rock up in a messy t-shirt or loads of modern jewellery'. The fourth rule is wear presentable clothes. Unless it's a very confident and deliberate choice on your part designed to suggest an aspect of the character, 'you don't want to look like you don't care about your appearance or presentation', an agent explains. Finally, as a casting director advises, 'don't wear anything that's going to make you uncomfortable or self-conscious'. One actor I spoke to gave an important example: 'Avoid colours that will show sweat patches!'

Follow those rules, making a choice from your everyday wardrobe that, as one actor describes, 'alludes to the part', or as a casting director phrases it, 'the essence of the part'. By very subtly giving a suggestion of the character's job, their characteristics or what you might sensibly assume they'll wear in the production, you'll gently help the casting team see you in the role and demonstrate you've put a little bit of thought into what you're doing. Plus, as one casting director points out, 'wearing something towards what the character is wearing may make you feel closer to the part'. A leading agent gives two simple examples to help: for the role of a business person in an office, 'don't wear a suit and tie, but choose something neat and smart that you'd normally wear'; if you're going for the young lead in a period drama, choose something 'light, plain and unfussy'. Other interviewees say different colours and cuts will help you appear older or younger then you are, if that's what's required. To prevent going too far in the wrong direction and heading towards costume, an experienced screen actor helpfully advises, 'ask yourself, "Could I go out for lunch with friends afterwards and not feel like I'm dressed like a dick?" '

If you're really struggling, one actor advises asking, 'What would my character wear out of my wardrobe?' Another told me that for roles from history they 'try to think about wearing the modern dress version of what the character would be wearing'. If you've still no idea what to wear for an audition, or don't have time to think about it, then one helpful agent says 'pick something neutral. That's always safe'.

When it comes to hair and makeup, use the same principles: subtly suggest character if you can but if in doubt go for something presentable that makes you feel confident. Interviewees suggest simple things are effective, with one actor explaining, 'I'll style my hair a little for a period part', and a director saying, 'if the character probably has stubble then grow it out for a day if you can. Women putting their hair up or down can make a big difference. It's those kinds of little things that work.'

Dry-running your audition

Several actors interviewed say they take up any opportunity to dry-run their audition, with one telling me, 'the aim of prep is so that you can walk in super-confident; I practise till I am'. There are various sugges-tions on ways to do this: in a class; with an acting coach; filming your audition self-tape style and watching back. This advice falls very much in the find-what-works-for-you category, with another actor explaining, 'I think it's possible to over-rehearse, and you can end up feeling pent up about what you'll be doing in the audition.'

Final checks

If you're taking a script or sheet-music in with you, make sure it's marked up and is easy to handle; you don't want to be dropping it everywhere or spending half the audition trying to find the right page. To avoid scrambling around seconds before you have to leave, get any props or any other bits and bobs you need sorted the evening before. And finally, if you're not sure, check in advance exactly where you're going, how you're going to get there and that your transport routes are running smoothly.

And … relax!

As one casting director advises, preparing for an audition is a balance between wanting to 'be great versus not stressing out'. Many experi-enced actors agree that finding a little time away from the script is an important aspect of the process: 'Part of preparing is about aiming to create relaxation'; 'I screw auditions up when I become really obsessive and micro-manage. I just get heated up, nervous and tense'; 'Learn what is excessive and be aware of when over-preparing becomes a bad thing'; 'You want to do everything you can, but not to the point of sleep deprivation.' If you're starting out, err on the side of caution here. After all, there's no point turning up fully zen but not having looked at the script, and you may find that preparing as hard as you can is the thing that relaxes you most! Over time, advice suggests you'll start to find the right balance; as an experienced actor says, 'you have to learn how *you* prepare'.

For free resources to help you make the most of the expert advice in this chapter, visit www.actorscareerbible.com/freestuff

11
ON THE DAY

Actor-interviewees say the auditioning experience can be anything from an invigorating, confidence boost to, at the other end of the scale, a draining ordeal. This chapter has lots of tips on how to make the process easier and give yourself the best chance. As one leading career coach says, 'auditions are the strangest thing to put yourself through ... but it's a part of your job to find ways around that.'

Use the advice in this chapter to work on:

- Using the hours before an audition

- Avoiding common mistakes in the room

- Keeping a level head afterwards

- Picking out lessons to learn for next time

Before the audition

It's impossible to know how you'll feel on the day. All you can do is create the best conditions possible.

Busy screen and stage actor

This section offers various ideas from interviewees on how to use the two or three hours before a meeting. Find what works best for you, which may well change from audition to audition.

Arrival times

For several actors, giving yourself time before a meeting starts is an important part of the process. 'I always get to the area at least an hour early,' one says. 'I find a quiet café nearby to allow the stress of the journey to fade and refocus my energies.' Another takes a similar safety-first approach, advising, 'know where there's a cafe near the audition and use their toilets to do final checks – you haven't got bits in your teeth or your flies aren't undone – without being flustered or distracted.' Another highlights the benefit of leaving plenty of time, saying audition venues often 'aren't clearly sign-posted; they can be in people's houses or small offices. Don't just think, "Alright, I've found the area or the actual road"; find the front door'.

Whether they get to the area early or not, most actors say they go into the audition itself ten to fifteen minutes before they're called. This gives them time to calm down and, as an actor highlights, 'is a chance to prepare if there is new material'. One performer, however, offers a more extreme approach: 'I never go in early. I get there bang on time, go straight in, do the audition and then get the fuck out of there. They're always running late anyway, and spending time with the competition can start to niggle and eat away at your confidence.'

A casting director explains what to do if ever you realize you're going to be late: 'Make sure we know. Call your agent who will call us. If you haven't got an agent, call the casting office. Things happen! We know there are travel difficulties, and that peoples' boilers break down. What's bad is wandering in two hours late with no reason.' Once you arrive, 'if you need a minute, take it; don't come into the audition room rushed and flustered'. And once you're in the room, 'say "Sorry I was late"' and do your best to carry on as normal: 'It's a waste of everyone's time if you can't then do a decent audition.'

Travelling to an audition

One successful screen actor advises making the most of your journey time, incorporating it in to your prep: 'Use the way you walk, the way you interact with the city, the music you listen to as a getting-into-character exercise, to get into another rhythm, physicality, mindset or accent.' Another told me, 'I use the journey to let off steam,' with several others saying that music, podcasts and books are useful distractions, and meditating or going over useful audition mindsets (see 'Handling nerves' below) can help. For others, the journey is a chance to do last-minute work on the script. 'I've given up trying to look sane on the way,' one actor admits. 'I'll mutter my lines to myself on the tube and in the street. Better to look eccentric than be unemployed.'

In the waiting area

The important thing in the waiting area is to 'understand what you need and be bold enough to do it', one actor says. For some this is simple; the waiting area is for last-minute line-learning and getting script and anything else you want to bring into the room organized. For others, however, it means thinking more carefully about how they interact. 'Do you respond better to keeping quiet and focusing … or to socializing and getting yourself in a place where you are responding?' one actor suggests asking yourself. Those interviewed take different approaches: 'I don't see the virtue of making small-talk'; 'If there's a possibility of being a little distant from other people then that's fine, if I feel like I need that'; 'You all end up at the same castings, and maybe a "We're all in it together" attitude is more useful than a "Fuck you" attitude.'

Some actors prefer to avoid the waiting area altogether: 'You've got nothing else to do except look at all the other people who are up for the same part as you,' is one performer's view. If you feel the same then, as mentioned previously, do your best to time your arrival. Alternatively, as another actor suggests, 'find any private space you can and use it', taking yourself off to warm up or run over lines. And if you really can't stand waiting one actor says, 'ask to pop out for a few minutes and come back'.

Handling nerves

Perhaps the most common advice when it comes to nerves is 'use them!' As one actor explains, 'that adrenaline is important. It's an old adage, but nerves are good!' While that's all fine, you'll want to limit nerves being a distraction, and beyond preparing thoroughly, the following pages list mindsets to practise that reduce the pressure around auditioning.

Frame auditions positively

Seeing auditioning as an unpleasant test doesn't help most performers, and casting directors I spoke to were unsurprisingly keen that actors focus on the more positive aspects of the process. The simplest way to do this, they say, is to remember auditions are a chance to act – the very thing we enjoy doing! Casting teams also highlight that every meeting is an opportunity to improve as a performer and get better at auditioning itself. Interviewees in general also encourage taking a positive view towards the panel. One actor suggests, 'think of them as your partner in the audition room … work with them', with another echoing this, explaining, 'I like the dynamic to be like I'm on set.' A film producer meanwhile says 'remember the reason you're in the room is because we want you to get the job … if you get it, then we don't have to see any more people and we can move on with the process.'

Accept the limitations

The audition process is designed with casting teams' needs in mind. It allows them to see enough actors in the small window they have during the production process, and it works because they're skilled at quickly picking out the information they need to make decisions. From an actor's point of view it therefore has inherent limitations: we're never likely to get a crystal-clear breakdown, as much time as we'd like to prepare and perform, or another go if we're not happy. We're not even guaranteed a warm welcome into the room, as casting teams deal with the pressure of trying to get the roles filled.

Rather than moan about the process – which builds negativity and gives you an excuse for not fully committing – it's freeing to accept these limitations. Auditions are not an environment where you'll necessarily feel like you've done your best work, nor are the performance conditions always going to give you a satisfying experience. Expecting these things creates pressure before and during, and almost inevitable disappointment afterwards. But lower your expectations and the pressure lifts; the challenge becomes not 'How do I give a brilliant performance?' but, as one performer describes, 'How do I give my best in the circumstances?' 'You may not have learnt the lines as thoroughly as you'd like or you may have been late,' another actor explains, '... still go for it!' Remember that you're giving a work-in-progress ('auditioning is not the same as a performance,' a casting director emphasizes), conditions are the same for everyone and that you can't change them. And if you come out and haven't enjoyed it, that's not necessarily an indication that it's gone badly; it's simply an occupational hazard.

Separate your job from theirs

A director explains how casting decisions are made: 'I'm not looking at a part in isolation. It's about who's been cast as the best friend, the boyfriend, the parent, how all that matches up. It can be about profile; I may have two people I can market the show with so for your part it now doesn't matter. A lot of it comes down to physical characteristics; if on the day I see them as short and you're really tall ... .'

Their advice therefore is as far as possible focus on *your* job and leave worrying about who's right to the casting team: 'Treat "getting the role" with abandon. There's so much outside of your control. All you can do is your best. At the end of the day, if I see a certain character a certain way and you're not that person there is nothing you can do about that. You can do everything you can possibly do to get in the room – and being prepared and being good really helps – but you can't suddenly become shorter or suddenly very well known.'

With this in mind, several interviewees suggest placing the meetings you get in their wider context. As a casting director advises, think of auditions 'as a general for that (casting team), for *all* their projects', while a career coach reassures, 'getting through the door means you have a real opportunity for the role *and* for the future'.

Remember you are always called in for a reason

Various actors interviewed described destabilizing thoughts popping into their heads before, during or after auditions such as 'I'm not right for this', 'It's going to a name' or 'I don't deserve to be here'. But, as one casting director underlines, it's vital you manage these thoughts and 'don't talk yourself out of a part'.

To help, another casting director advises reminding yourself that, 'if [a casting team] brings you in then it's likely we will have seen enough of you to think that you can do it'. An actor-producer meanwhile explains, 'when you see the process from the other side, you see they really think about it. They don't have a lot of time, and it's a given by that stage anyone coming into the room is going to be good.' And another casting director perhaps puts it most simply: 'We watch hours and hours of acting; trust us.'

During the audition

It's like meeting the in-laws for the first time. You'll be nervous, but you will try and be as charming as you can. And then, after that, it's something different ... it's acting!

                                                                        Film producer

Once in the room, an actor's job is fairly simple: greet the casting team, have a chat, listen out for direction, give your performance, say 'Thank you' and then leave. Complicating this process – worrying about 'audition technique' – is not necessary or particularly helpful. 'Caring less about tiny details is really important,' one experienced performer explains. 'This doesn't mean being blase or lazy. It means accepting a lack of control and not fixating on small things that probably won't matter.' The tips in this section therefore will help you avoid basic mistakes and put your preparation to good use.

Meeting the casting team

A key skill at auditions is the ability to take the unexpected in your stride, from the moment you walk in the room. Actors say the make-up of the casting team may be different to what you were told, and the room itself might not be what you're expecting: oddly small or big, with the casting team sitting alarmingly close or far away, or the camera right in your face or over the other side of the room.

It's important to be prepared for every possible type of reaction when you walk in. Much of the time, actors say you'll be greeted politely and the atmosphere in the room will be relatively relaxed. However, an experienced actor explains: 'you go sometimes and there's a weird vibe', and there were plenty of stories from other actors of casting teams that came across as nervous, disinterested or even rude. A performer offers some reassuring advice in this case: 'It's easy to see it as a reflection of their feeling about you but it is much more likely to be a reflection of their struggles with the casting process or just their personalities.' A producer meanwhile reveals they may not be as jolly as you'd hope, because 'there is pressure on them in the room … for the casting director to produce good options, and for everyone to find the right person. We need to find somebody, and that somebody has to say "Yes!"' The advice then is to 'just go with it', as another actor says. In fact, casting directors and experienced performers repeatedly highlight that you can work with the atmosphere in the room (positive or negative): 'Adapt to what's happening in front of you'; 'Judge the room and the personality of the casting director, just like you would in real life'; 'Make your judgement about how to behave from them, and perceive the way they want to connect to you.'

While you want to 'buy into the feeling in the room', as an actor puts it, another points out that sometimes 'your attitude can create their attitude'. One performer suggests meeting the panel with the positive mindset, 'I'm going to help them by being a good option', while another advises, 'you can dictate the tone by being gently positive, and by being yourself. This doesn't mean thinking, "I'm feeling shit so I'm going to tell them how shit I'm feeling." Leave negative things outside, even if it's just for five minutes. But try to be the best, most positive version of you you can muster. It's flicking that switch. If you have had a shit day it's reminding yourself before you go in that room that you're grateful for having this opportunity, you want to meet some new people, and they want you to have the job as much as you want to be the right person for them.'

Once you're in the room, 'if you're confident being talkative and making a connection then go for it, but know what you are comfortable with', a performer reassures. Casting teams say they like to see the 'normal' you (you'll hopefully be working together for the next however many weeks and months), so don't worry if you're not naturally gregarious. Plus, casting directors say that your personal qualities may be the thing that gets you the part, or they might be impressed by your transformation when you go into your reading. And while it's great if you can feel a sense that everyone's equal and you're also 'auditioning them', casting directors say it's natural to feel lower status sometimes (they have a job you want, after all), and they won't find it odd if you are quiet, polite and gently respectful.

Finally, one actor says it's sometimes worth considering what's most useful for your performance: 'If being chatty will make it difficult for you to switch back to the character's energy then wait till after the reading to chat and show your personality.' Another successful performer echoes this: 'If it is very clear what they are after, I'm going to go in from the start matching the essence of the character. You don't have to do anything spectacular. The character is cold and unpleasant; to match this character I wouldn't be unpleasant but I would be a little cold; I don't go in being gregarious and making jokes and all that.'

As the range of advice suggests, while you can simply try to be yourself, sometimes finding the right approach is a bit of a balancing act. 'You can dictate the tone in the room,' an experienced actor sums up, but 'sometimes they try to dictate the tone, and you have to let them.'

The interview/chat part of the meeting

Casting teams explain that any discussion in the meeting is there to help actors relax, to find out how the actor sees the role and allow for some initial direction and, as one casting director highlights, 'the director can get to know the actor; an actor might do a brilliant read but they may be horrible!'

Actor-interviewees say that as a general rule, theatre auditions will probably involve more chat (it's important for a director to understand who they're going to be spending four weeks in the rehearsal room with), whereas the first round of a TV audition is more likely to be about getting you on tape, especially if you're meeting a casting assistant. As always, there are no fixed rules, so don't be alarmed if you don't spend half your audition chatting away. The casting team may be in a hurry or have decided that getting to know you is not a priority at this particular stage.

The following pages list the most common topics that come up, with advice on discussing them. Use the guidelines but understand you don't need to pre-plan what you're going to say. As one actor highlights, 'when I first started auditioning I was incredibly conscious of saying the right thing. You eventually realize that people can sniff that out very very quickly.' Casting teams won't throw you trick questions and there are no right answers. The general advice is simply to keep an ear out for direction, give positive responses and don't rabbit on. 'Being a good listener really helps actually,' one director reveals. 'Some people, especially when they're nervous, can end up talking a lot.'

'What have you been up to?'

Generally, this question translates as, 'Tell me about some acting jobs you've been doing recently.' Answering is easy if you've been working on anything relatively impressive; even better, if what you worked on can be connected in some way to the project you're auditioning for.

But if you're currently out of work, don't worry. As one actor advises, you can 'use a phrase like, "I've just finished" … you can stretch that a bit if it was two or three months ago' (a phrase like 'recently' or 'most recently' also works well). If it's been a longer gap, an experienced casting director says, 'if it's something that you really enjoyed, even if it was eight months ago, then that's fine too – as long as you're upbeat'.

If you haven't got a job to talk about, then actors say anything acting related is fine. 'I see the question to mean, "Are you keeping busy and involved in the industry?"' an experienced screen performer explains. 'They're not asking, "Have you been sitting at home? Have you been going down Wetherspoons a fair bit?" I wouldn't say, "I haven't worked for ten months." But I would absolutely say, "I've just been directing a short film," or "I've just been running some acting classes."' Another actor suggests you could simply mention 'a play you've seen'; again, the more relatable to the project you're auditioning for, the better.

Alternatively, a casting director-interviewee advises you can say 'anything positive … "I've been doing some landscape gardening" or "I've been decorating my lounge". Everyone knows actors are out of work some of the time. Just come back with something that's not depressing and not, "Oh I haven't worked since 2016."' Another casting director reassures, 'honesty is fine, times have changed. It's generally an old-fashioned idea that if you have been out of work then you can't be any good. There's no shame in it.'

This approach may feel a bit risky for some actors, and the general advice is if you have a previous project you can mention, even if it's months and months ago, then that's going to be your best bet in most cases. Being more informal can work but assess the atmosphere in the room first. And when meeting major producers or directors, 'you have to judge it', says one actor. 'If you're sitting in front of Quentin Tarantino then you probably don't want to start talking about your waitering job.' As always, balance what's going to put you in a good place with an awareness of what the casting team will be comfortable with.

If you're in any doubt, you don't have to launch into an anecdote; vagueness is fine, as is very slight exaggeration, as long as you don't directly lie about anything or seem evasive. And you can rely more on how you say things, rather than what you say. Coming across as interested and engaged in the industry (and positive and confident about yourself) is going to be attractive, whatever your current situation. And finally, remember, as one casting director says, 'if you do a good reading and are right for the part, then they won't care that you haven't worked for a year'.

'What are your thoughts on the script?'

Any research and preparation you've done will obviously be of help here (see Chapter 10). The golden rule is don't criticize; 'if you can't say something nice don't say anything at all', a producer advises. At the same time, don't go all out trying to impress: 'Over the topness doesn't work. No one buys, "I luurrvvee the script."' They suggest that if you're not sure, be brief and keep things positive: ' "I really enjoyed reading it, thought it was great." '

Beyond this they advise, if you can, 'picking out something specific is much better and much more believable: "I really like the script and I love the way that she/he does this or says that." It shows you've actually read it and you understand something about it, it may be informative for them and you may have noted a moment that they are quite proud of as well.'

'What are your thoughts on the character?'

This is another area where good preparation will help. The advice here is, again, pick out something particular if possible. 'When you ask an actor about their character and they're able to say something specific you think, "Wow, they've really thought about this, possibly way more than I have." That can be impressive,' a theatre director reveals. However, you're warned against going into too much detail! As one actor points out, 'you don't want to say something completely away from what they may think', while another warns, 'don't set yourself up to deliver something ... and then not deliver it.'

Actors say this is also a good opportunity to pick up clues and discuss options if you're unsure. 'Initiate a dialogue at the beginning of the audition,' one successful performer advises. 'You could say, "I'm interested in the style of the piece, I think it could be done this way or that way," or "I think the characters are quite heightened," or "I imagined it like this," ... and then ask, "is there a particular style you have in mind?"' Meanwhile, a theatre director suggests, 'you can get a handle of the grey areas of the character by saying, "I had to make a choice about whether she's X or Y and I think Y because of this in the text ...".' They point out that as long as you're offering some ideas, 'at the very least I'll see you can make and justify choice, and I can then steer you in the right direction'.

Again, if you're in serious doubt, keep things simple: give short, positive answers. Casting teams say your performance will demonstrate your thoughts and choices much better than your words.

'Do you have any questions?'

If asked, bring up reasonable questions, like you would if you were on set or in a rehearsal room; especially if you haven't received all of the script or had very little time to prepare. As one actor advises, 'ask to help you understand the style and what they might be looking for. They are unlikely to think, "Oh, what an obvious question."'

Otherwise, casting directors often say this is just a convenient and polite way to get in to the reading or signal the audition is at an end. An experienced actor advises, 'if they ask you if you have any questions at the end of the audition and you don't, don't make one up. Just say "No, thank you, you've been really clear."'

Highlighting a link between you

'You can pick out links [with the casting team] – "I've just done X and I know you worked with actor Y,"' a coach explains, adding 'you'll be building rapport'. A successful actor agrees, saying, 'by displaying you've done some research you'll be making a good impression'. The advice is to don't crow-bar this in; ideally it should be within the natural flow of the conversation.

Complimenting their previous work

Although you're advised to be aware of the casting team's previous work, be wary about trying to butter them up. As one producer explains, 'it's quite discountable if someone comes in and flatters people about what they have done previously.' Instead, the advice is that this is fine if done in a confident, relaxed way or if it comes up naturally as part of the conversion. As always, being specific will be more impressive and make you appear more genuine.

Taking direction

Direction can come up between readings, but also in discussions you have before you do your first read. It's important, therefore, as one successful screen and stage performer explains, to 'keep your radar very open for their prompts and clues. Success or failure can come down to not listening enough.'

Interviewees say you can help yourself by preparing in a flexible way (see pages 145–146). Developing a positive attitude towards being redirected will also help, with casting teams and experienced actors alike advising you don't view notes as criticism. Instead, see direction as the casting team helping you and as a good acting challenge. Understand that there are various reasons why you might receive direction: to see if you can match how they view the role; to see how easy you are to work with; to see how adaptable you are; because they're not sure what they're looking for; because an idea has just popped into their head; or simply because they enjoy working with actors. The important thing is not to judge why; just listen closely and carry out their suggestions, however left-field. The information you pick up may contradict what was on the brief, what you've been told by an agent or what the script seems to imply. Accept this, and keep that radar open!

Performing in an audition

Always assume you're reading with the casting director, unless told otherwise. Some will give you very little, others might really go for it. The rest of the casting team may fidget, write things down and even appear to switch off. Experienced actors say the skill is in not treating the panel like a standard audience (they are doing their job) and reminding yourself that auditions are not a normal performance situation.

If you're interrupted early, casting directors emphasize you shouldn't see it as a criticism of your performance. Rather, they explain, they're reacting to what you're doing, finding new thoughts and directing the work. Listen, adjust and carry on. And once your reading has finished, do your best not to search for signs of approval. Casting teams all differ; they may be enthusiastic but equally they may keep their cards close to their chest. Again, your job at this point is to listen to any direction or clues they give on how to adjust your performance.

If you forget a line, a screen casting director advises: 'behave as if you were at work. Don't make excuses, ask for the line and carry on. This might even suggest you have some professional awareness.' If your reading falls apart completely then the same advice applies. 'Try not to show stress in that situation. If you feel it's really not going well, ask, "Sorry, do you mind if we start again?" Just don't do it if you're nine tenths of the way through!'

If you come to the end of your read, then another casting director says 'if you feel genuinely uncomfortable, you can ask to do it again; it's your ten minutes.' However, this is only advised as a last resort and if you're sure you could do something very different. 'Be careful not to push it,' one actor warns. 'I've learnt over the years to shut the hell up because it's never going to be perfect.' If you feel you have to ask for another read, their advice is, 'don't do it with negativity. Accept any positive comments they give you and don't make a face that says, "Oh that was rubbish" and be apologizing for it. That's the kind of attitude they might think you'll bring to the set.' Their final tip is if you have to ask, 'once is maybe ok … but don't take the piss and ask to do it four or five times again!'

After the audition

You have to recover and get better … because you have to go back into the room.

Experienced screen and stage performer

The advice in this section offers strategies so you not only 'have a plan in place for when auditions are disastrous', as one actor advises, but are able to keep a level head however you think you've done. Some of the tips here you may want to try straight after a meeting; others are useful or easier to deal with in the days or weeks beyond.

Letting go of the audition

Fixating on your audition afterwards is almost inevitable, with one performer interviewed saying wryly, 'whoever has the remedy of how to let go, please tell me'. Your aim therefore isn't to become totally zen about auditioning but, as our actor-interviewee puts it, 'to get better at letting go'.

If you feel you've had a bad audition, it's useful to remember you're not alone. 'There will be times when it goes badly and you were nervous or whatever. The next one will probably go swimmingly. That's just the way it goes,' one actor told me. Another says, 'Don't torture yourself. As long as you've done the work, you can say, "Ok, that is what happened today."' Casting teams themselves say a bad audition isn't fatal, and one director advises you keep some perspective: 'Think of acting as a career rather than an individual audition.'

As one career coach suggests, it helps to remember actors are normally a pretty poor judge of their own performance: 'When you think you've smashed it you've probably done too much; and when you're tired you may have been at your most natural and edgy.' Your inner experience – marked by nerves, adrenaline or even aspects of the character – will colour your view and means that your perception won't necessarily bear any relation to what the casting team saw or thought. This is borne out by the number of actors I spoke to who thought they'd bombed a meeting, only to get recalled, cast or seen again for another project a few months later. As one describes, 'I went home – cried – still got the job.' One actor points out the reverse can also happen: 'Sometimes you go in and you're told, "Thank you so much, that was really good, these are the dates, are you free?" ... and you still don't get it.'

With this in mind, do your best to avoid combing back through each second of the meeting, searching for hope or criticizing yourself. Accurately reading the casting team's reactions in the room is very difficult, and not just because of your perspective as an auditionee. Interviewees say that they may have rushed you through the meeting for reasons that have nothing to do with your performance: they have limited time, they saw you were good from your one read or you just weren't what they were looking for for this particular part. And as mentioned already in this chapter, they may have been cold with you because they're under pressure themselves or it's just the way they are as people.

Allow yourself time to feel frustrated, angry, elated or deflated if you need to (remember, it's perfectly natural). Actors suggest calling up a mate in the industry; have a good old moan and you might feel better. Others suggest if you're represented, speak to your agent. If you have this sort of relationship, an actor advises, 'keep a positive stance, but let them know about any feedback; even that the character wasn't right for you or you felt uncomfortable, that you felt a little off your game for whatever reason.'

Finding something to distract you is highly recommended. 'Another audition is the best way,' one actor says, but if not then another says, 'I do a bit of retail therapy or I'll go and eat a filthy burger ... congratulate myself. You put so much emotional energy in to getting prepped for this thing.' One actor's solution is to arrange to meet a friend: 'Seeing them makes me feel better, and you're forcing yourself into a social situation where you can't be in a bad mood and indulge.' Others suggest: 'meditation'; 'something that connects you back to the reasons you became an actor (a class or a show), what you really enjoy about acting itself, not just getting jobs'; and 'setting aside time for your own things' such as your second job, getting away for the weekend, seeing family or people unrelated to acting or working on other creative interests and projects. Working on other areas of you career covered in this guide might even be a good option!

Taking care of yourself is obviously also recommended, though, for some, a big blow-out might be the best solution ... do whatever works for you. One actor I spoke to hides their phone as often as possible for a few days so they're not constantly checking it. Another very deliberately bins their audition script when they get home – a closure ritual that helps them to move on to the next thing.

Finally, if you really can't move on, and have waited a reasonable amount of time (a week or so), one actor advises, 'if you really wanted something and you felt the audition went well, call your agent and ask for closure; you might get a nice surprise!'

Judge success on your own terms … and learn lessons for next time

Rather than spending your time and energy speculating about what the casting team may have thought of you, judge the success of your auditions on your own criteria, and pick out what you can work on for next time.

An experienced actor suggests you start by asking yourself, 'Were you in a good state when you walked in the room?' Did you:

- Prioritize the right areas to prepare?
- Give yourself enough time to prepare?
- Work hard enough in that time?
- Have everything you needed in place?
- Have a place you could properly focus?
- Get enough sleep, rest and relaxation?
- Organize your script and anything else you needed?
- Use your journey effectively?
- Arrive at a useful time?
- Arrive with a positive mindset towards the industry and the audition process?
- Manage any nerves that came up on the journey or in the waiting room?
- Behave in the waiting room in a way that helped you?

Then think about how you did in the room itself (based on things you can control):

- Did you greet the panel confidently?
- Was there anything unexpected that happened in the room that you can be prepared for in the future?
- Did you have positive answers for their questions?
- How about your reading? Were you able to adapt and deliver a good work in progress?
- How did you deal with direction? As one successful screen actor says, 'did you listen, think fast and make changes? So many

times in auditions they have said something to me, I wasn't thinking fast enough, and then I came out and thought, "Oh fuck, he
told me. He was telling me to be more passionate. Why didn't
I hear that?" '

- Were there any mindsets that hindered you in the room?

- Were you able to manage your nerves?

If you want to be super-efficient, go through these questions after every
meeting. However, just thinking generally in this way after an audition
can improve your mood and your chances of future success.

And take steps to improve where you can. For example, if you didn't
have enough time to prepare, try to get more flexibility in your second
job; if you felt nervous being among other actors in the waiting room,
think about adjusting your arrival time for your next meeting.

Keep a record of your auditions

Actors say that making a few notes after an audition will help you if you
get called in again by the same people and are useful when you have
a future performance to invite industry to. Make a record of who you
met, what it was for and anything that came up that might be worth
remembering.

If you don't get the role, some of the more resilient actors I spoke
to suggest going to see the production. 'Lots of actors don't do this
but it is a great learning platform,' says one very successful performer,
adding, 'it's great to see what the actor has done with the part and
the choices they have made. If they are amazing it will allow you to
accept the disappointment even more. If they're not great then you
can say, "Well you missed out." ' Their advice is that seeing the show is
also helpful 'if you audition for those people again' and it can be useful
for staying on their radar or if you want to get them along to see you
perform: 'Email with, "Really enjoyed auditioning for it. Saw it, loved it.
Doing this now." '

*For free resources to help you make the most of the expert advice in
this chapter, visit www.actorscareerbible.com/freestuff*

12
SELF-TAPING

If you're unprepared, self-taping – filming an audition in your own time and sending the video on to a casting team – can be, as one actor describes, 'really stressful, really annoying, and something that's going to ruin your weekend'. With guidance, however, you can quickly learn to do it with the minimum of fuss, taking the hassle out of another important aspect of your career.

Use the advice in this chapter to work on:

- Experimenting with your home setup and becoming comfortable with each aspect of the process
- Familiarizing yourself with other self-taping options

Self-taping at home

Experiment with your room and your lighting, so that you can then repeat. You will probably have to make minor adjustments each time you film, but you don't want to waste an hour setting up and testing.
Experienced screen actor

Making a good impression with self-tapes is about keeping things simple: 'We just want to see you framed and lit properly, and be able to hear you,' a casting director explains. To achieve this simplicity, an experienced actor reassures 'it's easy to spend very little to put together a home studio that looks like you've been in a casting office'. This section will take you through every step of the process – from deciding what equipment to use to sending your tapes off. Work on all this when you don't have an audition, so you can nail it when you do.

Camera equipment

Casting directors interviewed say that modern phones, tablets and laptops work perfectly for self-taping; in fact, an experienced performer told me 'I have an HD camera but often I just film things on my iPhone.' An extra that is definitely worth considering is a tripod, with more than one actor labelling them 'essential' if you're using a phone or tablet. You can buy reliable mini tripods online for less than £15.

The background

Don't shoot into the room; find a distraction-free background. 'A blank wall facing or adjacent to a window is best,' says one performer, with others I spoke to shooting against a blind, curtain or door; use whatever works in your home. A screen acting coach explains that 'black is not advantageous. White is great, or you go light blue, green, grey … any pastelly colour.' Avoid patterns, and anything else distracting, such as mirrors, paintings, photos, picture hooks or door handles. A further option is to buy something specifically for self-taping. An actor explains, 'I have a little roll-down blind. Go to IKEA or Amazon and buy something you can hook on to a wall or book frame.'

Positioning your camera

Make a decision about whether you're going to stand or sit, based on whatever's comfortable for you and works best for the scene. Your camera should then be in a fixed position, level with your eyeline. 'It has to be landscape', explains an experienced actor. 'If you film something portrait it does piss casting directors off.' A standard framing will include your shoulders and chest, with a small gap between your head and the top of the frame. As one actor explains, 'if there's a bit of movement make it a bit looser; go tighter in if it's a more intensely emotional'. Place your reading partner and any imaginary people and objects so your eyeline remains close to the edge of the frame.

Lighting your scene

Aim to have your face evenly lit and to cut out any overly distracting shadows on your background, while making sure there isn't so much light in the scene that it's glaring for the viewer. To achieve this, 'you don't have to be a professional photographer', an actor explains. 'You just have to move things around till they look less shit … or maybe even good!'

Start with your main light source. This should come from somewhere in front of you (otherwise you'll silhouette yourself) and at the same level or slightly higher than your eyeline (if it's coming from a very low position then you'll get odd shadows on your face). 'Natural light is very flattering', explains a successful self-taper. If you're shooting during the day in a room with a window, then if it's not too bright try facing the window directly (so the camera is between the window and you); if you want something less bright, sit at a more adjacent angle.

If you can't get enough natural light then don't rely on a ceiling light; 'you're gonna look like crap', explains one actor helpfully. As another screen actor advises, 'use a lamp. A basic IKEA one you can tilt and rotate a bit is absolutely fine; behind and above the camera, facing down, tilted in to the eyes'. If you're getting shadow on the wall behind you raise your lamp, and it will lower the shadow out of the frame (you may have to raise it up on a table or something similar to find the best position).

If you're having trouble with background shadows or struggling to get both sides of your face lit, then add a second light source; place a lamp on the opposite side to where your main light is coming from. For example, if your main light is a lamp, then as a screen director explains, arrange your second one 'so they're shining at you diagonally from either side'.

For an advanced setup, consider LED camera or soft box lights. These can be 'very flattering' says one actor, with another explaining 'they cost (from) £30 online'.

Sound

The closer you are to the camera, the better the sound quality will be. You want your voice to be the most audible so, as one actor advises, 'if your reading partner has to be closer because they're operating the camera, make sure their volume is lower than yours'. The mics on most phones and laptops are considered good enough, but 'if you have money to invest, buy a clip-on or directional microphone', one performer suggests. 'They make a big difference and only cost about £20.'

If you're lucky, you'll have absolutely no background noise on your tape. However, the nature of self-taping means that this isn't always possible, and as one casting director reassures, 'if the odd noise creeps in don't worry too much'.

Your reading partner

Ideally you'll have someone to help you film your scene and to read the other parts. 'Try if you can to get another actor,' says one casting director, explaining, 'sometimes the person reading in is so appalling'. A fellow actor can also keep an eye on technical aspects and might be able to offer you the odd directorial note. One performer advises, 'Always say "Yes" if others ask you, and you can store up the favours.'

If you have to rope in a non-actor friend or family member, then keep their read simple and quiet. Alternatively, some actors I spoke to film with their agent at their offices. If you have this option, then take it up; they'll probably have a good-looking setup, you can get their notes and they'll send it off for you; plus, it's a chance to build your relationship! And if you really can't find someone, then as a last resort actors recommend recording the other parts on another device.

Slating, title-cards and editing your tape

Slating is a way of introducing your tape by filming yourself looking directly into the camera (you can do this and then go straight into a scene or do it as a separate shot cut into the beginning of your tape). The advice here is that you only really need to slate-to-camera if the casting team asks you to (they will include instructions in an email, so check it carefully; if you're represented, ask your agent if you're unsure). If they don't ask, then you can choose to insert title-cards or onscreen titles; an option if you're doing lots of scenes or you just want a very well-labelled video. However, as one casting assistant says, title cards are 'quite helpful but not a necessity'. Instead you can include all these details in the labelling/message sections when you send your tape.

A typical example of a slate-to-camera would be:

- You saying, 'Hi, my name is Rosa Smith, I'm represented by John Brown at the Agent Agency, and this is Character X from Project Y'
- If asked by the casting team, zoom out or cut to a full-length face-on shot of you, and you turning to show profiles

A typical example of a title-card inserted slate (white font on a black background) would read:

Rosa Smith
Rep: John Brown@The Agent Agency
Character X in Project Y

Onscreen titles can simply be your name, the character name and scene number over the first few seconds of your tape/each scene.

To add title-cards and onscreen titles, one actor and editor explains simply import your tape to 'iMovie or a native editing app on your phone or laptop'. You can also then add any other finishing touches: chop anything unnecessary at the beginning and end of your tape, add fade-ins and fade-outs, link separately filmed scenes together or add title-cards between scenes (e.g. 'Scene 1', 'Scene 2' etc.). Beyond this – assuming you know what you're doing – they add, 'you can put on a grade or filter in iMovie'. If you're not confident, try clicking on the iMovie magic wand button, or leave this step.

Sending your tape off

DO NOT send the file directly by email. Instead, familiarize yourself with services like WeTransfer or Vimeo, both commonly mentioned by the casting teams and experienced actors I spoke to. Vimeo is recommended by one actor as 'more user-friendly', while a self-tape studio owner says 'a basic Vimeo account will allow you 500 Mb a week, which is enough for at least one tape a week'. The downside with Vimeo is you have to pay for Vimeo Plus for your tapes to be download-able at the other end (some agents and casting directors will ask for this). The upgraded version has several other benefits including faster upload times and more storage, so one actor advises, 'if you're getting a lot of self-tapes then it's easier to go with Plus'. Whichever service you prefer, always check casting team's emails to see if they've stated a preference.

One occasionally important step with WeTransfer and other file-shar-ing services is to compress (reduce the file size) your tape before send-ing. An experienced actor explains, 'casting directors tend to ask for files to be under a certain size because it's easy for them to download'. It also works out easier for you: 'With a bad internet connection, a 400 megabyte clip can take hours to upload, but a hundred megabytes will take 12–15 minutes.'

The head of a self-taping studio says, 'there's no fast and hard rules' when it comes to compression. 'If you're using Vimeo, there really is no restriction on the file size. With WeTransfer, anything between 100–200 Mb is usually absolutely fine these days, unless the casting director's got slow internet speeds.' As with other aspects of self-taping, their advice is: 'it's really about experimenting. Film something that's not a tape and try to export it to see what works for how you'd like to do it; try a level of compression and see how does it look, how does it sound?' An experienced self-taper suggests you can test quite a high level: 'You can probably lose two thirds of the size without losing any of the quality.'

A busy actor outlines several ways to reduce your file size:

- 'Drop your phone's camera resolution' (go to settings and choose 720)
- 'Use a compression app' (such as Compressor for iPhone)
- 'When you export your file from iMovie you'll get options – Small, Medium, or Large'
- 'If you're using Vimeo [the casting team] are given a few choices of size they can download it'

Label your tape before finally sending it. Check the casting team's email for instructions, but if not, include your name, your agent (if you're represented), the character and the project. If you're using Vimeo, then, 'check your option for a screenshot', advises one actor. 'Don't have one of you looking like a zombie, because that's the first image that the casting director will see. And do a password protected link; this will be seen by your agent and the casting director so don't put anything stupid; something related to the show is good.' Finally, if using Vimeo Plus, always click the box that means your tape's downloadable.

If you're new to self-taping and represented, actors recommend sending your tape to your agent, unless instructed otherwise. This will mitigate against any mistakes, they can offer you notes and, as an experienced self-taper outlines, 'if I can't decide between two takes I'll send them both to my agent and ask "Which would you pick?" '

Improving your self-taping

Working on self-taping without the pressure of an audition is a great practice for actors early in their career. Some performers I spoke to suggest going back over old audition scripts or finding new ones online to experiment with. Alternatively, you can work with a coach or try a self-tape course. Puro Casting's 21-Day Self-Tape Challenge was highly recommended by more than one performer; an affordable way to quickly improve your setup and confidence.

Other self-taping options

The Shoot Me! app – recommended by several interviewees for this guide – is designed to make the whole self-taping process easier by offering features such as light adjustment and filters, plus an easy editing, compression and file-sharing process. It's free, so you can experiment with it and see if it works for you.

Another option is to use a studio (e.g. Self Tape House or Bespoke Reels, both recommended by experienced actors) that will do the whole thing for you. The downside is obviously the cost, which means for most actors starting out this isn't an option they can use every time. However, if you have the budget, one happy actor told me: 'you get someone who's savvy with their knowledge of equipment and filming and who'll give good direction and be good to read off'.

And by leaving all the technical stuff in someone else's hands, you can just concentrate on the acting. One actor I spoke to says they use a studio if it's 'a particularly important audition', while another performer described them as 'a safety-net' whenever they can't find a friend to help them.

For free resources to help you make the most of the expert advice in this chapter, visit www.actorscareerbible.com/freestuff

PART FOUR

UNEMPLOYMENT AND MONEY

13
DEALING WITH UNEMPLOYMENT

This chapter shares advice on sustaining yourself mentally and financially during a period of unemployment and getting back to work as quickly as possible. The tips here will also help you put in place the foundations of a lifestyle and pattern of income to sustain a long career in an up-and-down profession.

Use the advice in this chapter to work on:

- Keeping buoyant mentally

- Staying afloat financially

- Giving yourself the best chance of getting back into acting work

---

Keeping buoyant mentally

Being an actor is a lifestyle, not just a job.

Screen and stage performer

The following pages describe common mindsets and habits suggested by actors and industry figures to keep you relatively calm during periods out of work in your first years in the profession.

Accept unemployment as part of the job

'It's inevitable', a leading agent told me when asked about actor unemployment. 'Everyone goes through it in some form or another. Even our actors who are doing really well, who are names, go through several months where they don't work.' Accepting and preparing for these periods out of acting work – rather than hoping you'll be lucky – is a key step in helping you to minimize any negative impact. As one seasoned actor suggests, 'more young actors need to take on the notion that they will have to survive the business'.

It's also useful to understand that it's completely normal to feel down during these periods. As a successful (yet still occasionally out of work) actor says, again part of the solution is to 'learn to accept that there will be emotional and mental costs to being an actor; the price you have to pay to give yourself a chance in a career that you want to be involved in'.

Hold on to the positives

However, unemployment doesn't have to be all doom and gloom. Actors point out that occasionally, 'resting' can come as a welcome break, especially if you've been on a long or not particularly happy acting job, or you've been away from home for a time. Some I spoke to see being out of work as a time to catch up with friends and family, pursue other interests or just relax. Others say it's a chance to tackle important aspects of their career, with one productive performer saying, 'I use it to do the things that need doing; accounting, photos etc.' If you sort out the 'things that need to get done', as they put it during quiet periods, then when an audition does come around, you'll be able in a position to give it your full focus. And over the longer term, by being productive in your early years in the profession, you can insure yourself against any leaner periods later in your career.

Plan

'Don't just stumble out of an acting job,' a successful screen performer advises. 'Make it look like you're ready for the next one!' They encourage you to plan your own mini-relaunch back into the profession. 'Freshen everything up if it needs it – photos, CVs and showreel – and polish up your skills. Contact your agent, arrange a meeting, and get the word out there that you're available now.' They also advise you email your own contacts: 'Cast the net back out there; don't assume people would have seen or known about (your last job).' Part of your plan should also be about finding second jobs: 'You have to consider the financial side of things. Be realistic. Think to yourself, "I don't think I'm going to work [as an actor] for a while now; this is what I'll do." '

This advice also applies to actors who are leaving training. If you're a final year student, give yourself some time to think about your transition into the profession. Take advantage of the guidance from your course staff and the tips in the rest of this guide so you're as prepared as possible in each aspect of your career (see the flow chart in the 'Using this guide' section for a breakdown of everything you can work on).

Create a life outside of acting

An experienced actor interviewed admitted, 'I found myself so stressed by unemployment that even when I was working I wasn't enjoying it; I was thinking about what would happen when the job stopped.' After many years of this, they eventually realized that 'I was expecting all my psychological needs to be met by acting … but of course as soon as the acting job finished, the rest of my life was a bit of a mess. I had no feelings of control, I had no money; all the relationships I had were tied up in theatre and if I wasn't working, I'd just sit at home alone or in a shitty temp job with people I didn't know; and I wasn't being creative or using any of my skills.'

Their hard-won advice is that it's vital you 'make a life that you like, that you're looking forward to getting back to every time you finish this brilliant job. That you can still find a sense of autonomy or control in your life, a sense of relatedness [warm supportive relationships and a feeling you belong] and of competence [you're doing something creative, using your skills to pursue something important to you].' Other performers echoed this when asked what gets them through a period of unemployment: opportunities to act; engagement in the industry; a separate creative outlet; progress towards getting auditions and acting jobs; a relatively reliable income; time for rest, relaxation and fun.

Ask yourself if your life outside of acting jobs is giving you what you need to be happy. If you're at a very early stage of your career, you may be able to cope more easily. But as your career continues, the advice is to work on creating those elements listed to build a fulfilling life outside of acting. This will not only stave off many of the common problems associated with acting unemployment, it will also help you make a better impression at castings; as one career coach highlights, 'being engaged, positive and attractive ... you have to create these things in yourself'.

Developing a routine, however gentle, will guarantee you have at least some of the important elements in place. There were lots of simple suggestions from actors of what you can build into a routine including: taking acting classes; setting time aside for marketing yourself; collaborating on creative projects; interests outside of acting; a second job or sideline career; time with friends and family; exercise; a set sleeping pattern; watching theatre, film and TV.

Pick out things to do that work for you, and if you're struggling with a problem – for example, if you're feeling cut off from the industry – build something into your routine to address it. You can create full-on daily or weekly schedules, or keep things really simple. One actor told me their only rule is to 'get out and about' at least once during the day: 'Nipping out to a coffee shop or getting outside gives me a change of environment, a bit of interaction and some fresh air.' Another told me that their routine is simply, 'Don't stay in bed all day; don't stay up late at night.'

Develop patience

Unemployment makes great demands of an actor's patience and there are tips throughout this guide on how to cope better, whether it's waiting for a response to direct contact, for your agent to call or for an audition result.

On a broader scale, having patience with your progress is a vital trait. 'Things won't happen as quickly as you think they will, and actors can be heavily demoralized by this,' a career coach acknowledges. 'But you are doing the right things! It just takes longer than you realize.' A successful and seasoned actor also encourages you to take a long-term view: 'It is really important to know that early "failure" – not being immediately successful and facing some struggles – is a possibility. [An

acting career] isn't about the next two years, or the next three years …
it's about the next 45 years, please god!'

Developing some ease with the ups and downs of the profession will
allow you to enjoy the 'journey', as one actor puts it. A career coach
explains, 'you don't have much autonomy over your careers, so you
need to embrace the excitement of uncertainty,' with an experienced
actor echoing this: 'Embrace the madness! Don't see [quiet periods]
as nothing on the horizon. Instead think, "Anything can happen!"' Their
advice is to 'work hard for everything and see how it shakes out. There
are no mistakes. You never know what anything will lead to. Things that
appear to be terrible or great may turn out to be the opposite. That
workshop that was seemingly dead-end somehow leads to you developing it into amazing work five years later.'

Key to developing patience is maintaining your belief: 'There is a
place for every good quality actor, and there will be opportunities at
some point,' a leading agent reassures, while an experienced casting
director says, 'if you're good enough – or make yourself good enough –
then you will get those opportunities. You might not become a film star
but you can become a rock-solid working actor.' An agent's assistant
perhaps best describes the mindset to work towards: 'You've got to be
confident that it's what you want to do and that you can do it, even at
rock-bottom points. Confidence in a realistic way. Not going, "I'm the
dog's bollocks," but knowing what you are good at, and that if you work
in a certain way you can get results.'

Limit career-envy

'It's great to have successful friends,' one actor told me. 'It normalizes
it, and it's inspiring and encouraging … but it's also hard at times.'
Experiencing some career-envy seems to be part and parcel of being
a performer, with every actor I spoke to admitting they'd felt it at some
point. A busy actor describes one simple strategy to help: 'Remind
yourself of your achievements. People always compare upwards, they
never compare downwards. It's easy to compare with peers who experience great things but imagine how many people want to be doing
what you're doing right now, or to have done what you've done.'
Another successful actor advises practising a positive attitude, even if
you're feeling envious: 'Send a note or call them, especially if you have

auditioned against them. You'll make them feel great, build your relationship and you'll be more comfortable with not getting things.'

Enjoy it!

One experienced showreel editor I spoke to emphasized the importance of not 'stressing about the minutiae' of every decision you make
as you build your career. They had observed over years of working
closely alongside industry figures and actors that 'this business can
make people extremely nervous and extremely introspective on a
destructive level, where they worry so much about everything they're
doing. The people who seem to make the best progress are the ones
who find themselves comfortable with where they are and where they
want to go; and they take a realistic view of how they're going to do
that. If you just enjoy the process and try to recognize that you got
into this business because you love it, not because you want to stress
about it, then that will come through in your work, in your tapes, in the
way you approach showreels and headshots, in the way you present
yourself and the way you engage with casting directors when you go in
for meetings. People will like you, and they will see you are in it because
a) you're talented and b) you enjoy it ... not because you're trying to
constantly push yourself somewhere that you shouldn't be.'

Build resilience

'The business side of the industry can seem shallow and cruel,' an
experienced performer told me, while another spoke of facing many
'knock-backs', and even at times being 'treated like a piece of meat'.
It's understandable in the face of this that actors sometimes find it hard
to stay motivated.

Part of building resilience is to practice framing 'No's and rude or
dismissive treatment as another normal part of being an actor. As one
career coach highlights, 'it's not your rules'; you can't change the industry, so you have to remain as objective as possible. In tough times, couple this with holding on to 'what you adore about this', urges one actor,
'so you don't get poisoned by that stuff'. The advice throughout this
guide also encourages you to always judge your efforts (rather than your
results) and focus on lessons you can learn for your next opportunity.

And, however bad things get, as one performer says, remember that 'when you do get the opportunity to work, the positives (of being in the profession) massively outweigh the negatives.'

Develop self-reliance

'Some actors have an idea of what they want to do but they don't seem to be doing that much towards making it happen,' an experienced casting director observes, and many go-getting performers seem to agree: 'You are never unemployed, you still have a job to do'; 'You have to take responsibility ... no one else will'; 'You need that ability to take care of yourself and not wait for others to deliver for you'; 'Despite agents and everything else there is a lot that you have to organize ... accounting, promotion, the work itself, side projects and (second) jobs.'

As our experienced casting director summarizes, 'when you face problems, rather than blaming others and outside factors, learn to look objectively at your situation, and where *you're* contributing to your own problems'.

Stay afloat financially

> *If you can find a second job that pays enough, is fulfilling and flexible then you have solved one of the biggest problems of being an actor.*
> Actor in the early years of their career

Taking on a second job is for most actors a necessary part of being in the profession. 'It's five percent of actors who don't have to have some-thing else going on,' an experienced performer estimates, with another relatively busy actor revealing, 'people assume you've done a bit of TV work and you're rolling in a bed of money ... you're not. A woman came up to me at my second job and said, "I saw you on telly the other night, why are you here?" ... Well, because I'm a jobbing actor!'

The advice over and again therefore is to tackle this area of your career head-on: 'No one wants to hear advice saying, "What else are you going to do?", because you think, "No, I'm going to make it! I never really listened to all that till I was five years out and having a dark patch, but it's so true, have that other thing!'; 'Find three other ways to get some money in, cos you are going to need them … now, and even more when you are 50 cos you might have a mortgage and kids and who knows what else'; 'If you're relying on an acting job or tax rebate popping up then there might be a problem. Acting can tide you over for a few months but you can't guarantee the next one coming in and you need to earn money to survive. There's no reason to be awkward or embarrassed about it'; 'When I'm acting I'm acting; when I'm not, I make as much money as I possibly can doing boring jobs.'

While second jobs of course can be 'boring', you aren't condemned to stay in an awful, low-paid position forever. The advice is to keep aiming for better options over time; as one actor says, start out with 'any job you can bear and go from there'.

Making second jobs more bearable

'There's no point sugar-coating it; at times [working a second job] will be tough,' an actor admits. Like many, their advice is to focus on the upside: 'See it as the price you pay for chasing a cool career!'

There are many other ways to frame things positively. A common tip is to see second jobs as a way of facilitating your career; the money funds your progress as an actor. Other benefits brought up by interviewees include: 'It gets you out of your acting-head for part of the day'; 'I was meeting actors, and you do make connections'; 'It's a chance to see some "real life"'; '[The money gives you] a nice life when you're not acting. Working for seven hours a day so that you can buy some nice shoes is better than sitting at home for seven hours, eating a tin of cold beans.' Others point out that some second jobs can be challenging and interesting in themselves. Plus, of course, if it's a job you really enjoy, you have the option to turn down any acting work you're not completely sold on!

Everything is more bearable if you can easily free up time for auditions and other opportunities that come up. 'Don't tie yourself in to anything with regular hours,' one performer warns. 'It's a recipe for headaches.' Choose a job with flexibility: shifts you can cancel or swap or get cover for at short notice, a position you can leave for an hour or two during the day, or hours mostly at evenings and weekends. If you're represented, couple this with being open with your agent, with one actor advising, 'talk to them – "I'm going to be working as much as possible at the moment." They may be able to swap (audition times) around.'

Be prepared to work hard and stay organized to keep yourself going. A now-successful actor describes their tough schedule at the beginning of their career: 'I come from a working-class background, I don't have wealthy parents or whoever to subsidize my income or bail me out. To make ends meet, I would do 9–5 from home remotely on my laptop, then pack it up, get a bus into town and do an evening shift in a bar … for weeks and weeks and weeks on end.'

At the same time, as one astute actor advises, 'be wary of how much your job demands of you'. While you may have to work hard at times, the advice is you can offset some of the negative effects by ensuring your second job isn't the main focus of your day. One experienced actor reflects, 'I sometimes felt hopeless, that I was wasting my life. But I coped by focusing on the fact that it's keeping the wolf from the door, and that it's close to my house. I can go home, and then till 10 pm I can really get on with something else.'

If you've just started your job and already feeling down, the advice is to give it time. Actors say the first days and weeks can be the worst, as you cope with no longer having acting work and find yourself in unfamiliar surroundings. Deciding on your attitude can also help. Some I spoke to choose to put in lots of effort, however menial the tasks involved, giving them a sense of satisfaction and reward, and creating a useful distraction from the industry-related chatter in their heads. Others recommend the opposite approach, doing the bare minimum, having fun with colleagues and making the most of breaks. You can switch your approach from job to job, or even day to day, depending on what's most likely to get you through.

Another way to take the pressure off is to be careful with your earnings when you have an acting job. 'Don't be frivolous … save!' an actor advises. 'You need to be sensible at times, as boring as that might sound. You get an acting job and think, "Great, I'll be alright for a couple of months," but that money will soon go.' And if you're not earning enough from an acting job, another actor says, 'don't feel bad that you're putting in a shift somewhere in the afternoon and going to do a show in the evening. It's the uncomfortable economics of being an actor for most people'.

Finally, one actor describes an alternative approach: rather than diving straight back into work after an acting job, they give themselves a short break. 'I didn't want to get £8.50 an hour to do a job that is going to make me really depressed, and then not have felt in a good place for auditions. I worked out that if I didn't have any luxuries, I could live on this small amount of money I had from acting. I went to the gym, ate well, relaxed, stayed calm and I was in the best state possible for meetings … and I got an acting job!' This approach obviously only works if you're certain you can afford it, and 'if you have discipline to use the time productively', as our actor-interviewees highlight. 'What will make you calmest?' they add. 'Is it worth living frugally, not desperately scrapping for a job, but instead using the time to actually look for a job that works for your lifestyle? A lot of actors don't acknowledge their bodies and their minds enough when they should actually just take a step back and organize their lives. If you can survive on the breadline a bit, sometimes it can be beneficial.'

Finding the right second job

A good second job needs to pay enough, offer flexibility and have a limited mental and physical negative impact on you as a performer. The jobs suggested in this section offer each in varying degrees, with two main types listed: shorter term, quick fixes and second careers. Use the advice to make choices to suit your current career stage, situation, lifestyle and personality.

Most actors I spoke to found jobs through friends, though many recommend putting the word out on Facebook and joining actor-related groups. Searching on Twitter was also suggested, as was using casting sites, listing sites like Arts Jobs online and going to events like Surviving Actors. If you've trained and live close to your drama school/uni then see if they offer any jobs. Or you can simply google something like 'jobs for actors' and loads of suggestions will come up.

Examples from interviewees of shorter-term jobs and quick fixes include bar and restaurant work, catering and promotions, ushering, call centre jobs, tutoring, nannying, temping and retail. Lots of actors do these types of jobs throughout the early years of their careers. They're relatively easy to pick up and drop, and normally offer flexibility. The downside is that they often aren't particularly fulfilling, aren't paid particularly well and getting enough hours can be tricky while fitting in auditions, classes and everything else.

As a result some actors pursue a second career that works alongside being a performer. If you're at an early stage in your acting career and have the time, money, motivation (and possibly existing skills) this can be a great choice, and something to begin working on as soon as possible. If you're further into your career, one actor says, 'you'll know when you are bored and exhausted of working in call centres and pubs; you have to start making a change when that point kicks in.'

As one performer explains, a second career that's acting-related 'massively helps. A corporate [for example] isn't anyone's dream job but it's useful, it can develop you; and it doesn't feel like working in a cafe'. Another experienced actor encourages performers to 'think of all the things you can do because you have this acting training and skills. We all want to work at the National, but that's out of your control. Instead, widen your definition of success to include anything that falls under the umbrella of "creative"'. Examples from interviewees of acting-related second careers include: voice-over (although not always easy to get into, lots of actors recommend investigating this option as early as possible in your career. Either record a reel and approach agencies or use online bidding sites); corporate role-play; workshop leading; drama coaching; showreel editing; headshot photography; assisting casting directors and agents; administration jobs at theatres, arts organizations and drama schools.

For others, a second career completely unrelated to acting works best, with one actor-interviewee explaining, 'nobody wants to be constantly reminded of what they'd rather be doing.' There's no limit here to what you might choose, as long as you can create some flexibility. I spoke to actors who are also personal trainers, masseuses, painter-decorators, or have their own businesses they run off their laptops. If there's something where you already have qualifications and/or an interest in, investigate whether it's a viable second career. Otherwise, search online for suggestions related to your interests and ask around among the actors you meet.

Give yourself the best chance of getting back into acting work

Keeping going is one of the most important things; make sure you keep going.

Career coach

While trying to stay relatively upbeat and organize yourself financially, actually doing something towards finding an acting job can accidentally drop down the priority list. Follow the tips here to stay on track.

Don't neglect your marketing

Several actors I spoke to set themselves goals to prevent neglecting work towards their chosen career. One told me they'd been advised by a highly successful industry figure to 'do something productive towards their career every single day', and other actors gave plenty of examples of simple daily tasks, from watching an episode of a TV drama, to searching through theatre websites or reading part of a play. Alternatively, you can work towards weekly aims (reading a whole play, for example, or applying for three jobs) or monthly goals (searching for and attending a workshop or researching and applying to agents).

Other actors set up basic rules to ensure they're getting something done. Examples include going no longer than three weeks without initiating some contact with their agent; at the beginning of each month booking two plays to go to; spending one weekday morning sending off industry emails; and setting aside half an hour at the end of the month to process receipts.

You can apply this thinking to other elements of your unemployment routine; from how often you exercise to making sure you're following interests outside of acting. It doesn't necessarily matter if, as one actor describes it, 'life gets in the way' and you don't end up achieving everything you set out to. The important thing is that you're putting yourself into some action that could help your career.

Ready yourself for auditions

An industry-leading agent advises you to use unemployment to 'get in a position where you can give 100% to your one audition a week, a month or a year'. With this in mind, begin tackling as soon as possible anything that's been holding you back. A recent and busy graduate gives the example, 'if you're always going up for the same accents then you need to practise them so you can nail those future auditions.'

You can ease the pressure come audition-time by following the approach of this actor: 'It's much better to maintain a general pattern that contributes to your success; a little-and-often approach rather than a binge effort every time you get a meeting. The week and day (before a meeting) mustn't lead up to this huge exam or job interview. Turning the audition into a big deal, a special moment, rather than part of a general lifestyle, creates tension. Suddenly you're going to bed especially early, which usually still means a sleepless night anyway, getting up really early, stretching, going to the gym, eating incredibly healthily, having a load of coffee … all these things signal to you that you are going into a high-pressure situation.'

There's lots of things you can apply this 'little-and-often' approach to sorting:

- Your major selling points (see Chapter 1), especially building confidence in your ability and maintain your skills and accents

- Clothes, shoes, makeup etc. you can use for auditions. Casting directors advise checking what you already have to cover your various casting types and filling in any gaps when you can if necessary. Keep everything presentable so they're ready to be used with very little notice

- 'Being in your look', as one casting director phrases it, is an area for some actors to consider. The advice is that if aspects of your look are a major part of your casting, keep to a sustainable routine; otherwise, you can find yourself rushing around before an audition trying to get a last-minute haircut or, as one actor describes, 'panicking because you've now got to go on a three-day diet and hit the gym'

- Increasing your engagement in the industry. 'What have you been doing recently?' is a common question casting teams ask at auditions. But as one cheery performer suggests, 'if you keep busy and proactive then you don't have to lie!'

- Checking in on your general mental state and attitude towards the industry. As a top career coach notes, one of your aims when things are quiet is to keep yourself 'match fit, psychologically and physically'

- Making sure you can easily get hold of scripts. As one casting director says, 'part of your job is to have everything up and running: your printer working, your phone bill paid, your internet reliable'. They also advise 'you have an alternative if anything goes wrong'. Find out where your nearest internet cafe, library or friend with a printer is. If singing is listed on your CV, then have a song and the sheet music ready for accompaniment. The same goes for monologues; if they're required for the castings you're submitting for, have a range learnt and work on them during gaps to save you stress come audition time

For free resources to help you make the most of the expert advice in this chapter, visit www.actorscareerbible.com/freestuff

14

TAX AND SELF-EMPLOYMENT

As one actor-interviewee helpfully explains, 'tax takes up time and it's boring'. The tips in this chapter – from accountants, Equity and a range of experienced actors – will show you how to confidently sort out tax and other aspects of self-employment, freeing up your time for the more interesting aspects of your career.

Use the advice in this chapter to work on:

- Getting your head round what you need to know
- Understanding what to do, when

What you need to know

To understand it is your first aim.

Actor, ten years in the profession

This section explains how to register for self-employment with HMRC (the government's tax-collecting department). You'll also learn all you need to get started with tax, National Insurance (NI) and student loans.

Tax years

The first thing to get your head round is tax years. Tax, NI and student loan repayments are calculated over a 12-month period, starting from 6th April each year and running through to 5th April the following year. So, for example, the 2019/2020 tax year will run from 6 April 2019 to 5 April 2020 inclusive.

Self-employment

Actors are classed as self-employed for any paid acting work they do. This means that tax, NI and student loan repayments related to acting jobs are calculated and paid at the end of the tax year. This is as opposed to PAYE (Pay As You Earn) jobs, such as working in an office or a bar.

Expenses

An allowable expense is anything you've paid for that is clearly related to you doing your job as an actor. The idea is you add up your expenses over the tax year, and that total then reduces the amount of income you have to pay tax on.

Working out expenses is not always an exact science. The basic rules are:

- Include the total cost of an item or service if it's entirely related to your acting: for example, agent fees

- Some expenses are both for acting (or 'business') use and for personal use. For these you should calculate or estimate the percentage related to your acting; for example, for your mobile phone bill, you might estimate that only 30 per cent of your total bill of £500 over the tax year is related to acting use, therefore the expense totals £150

- In your first tax return you can include your 'startup costs' as expenses. These are anything acting-related you paid for before you registered for self-employment: for example, a Spotlight subscription or first set of headshots

If you have an accountant, they will advise you on what and what not to include. The most common categories of expenses for actors are:

- Fees related to acting: for example, agent commission and VAT on that commission, accountancy fees, Equity subscriptions, casting site subscriptions

- Headshot, showreel, voice reel payments

- Theatre and cinema tickets

- Industry-related website, magazine and newspaper subscriptions

- Payments for acting seminars, talks and networking events

- Office costs related to acting: for example, stationery, postage, printing costs

- Books, downloads, sheet music, etc. for auditions, rehearsal or performance

- Costume you've paid for to wear solely in performances, auditions or classes, and the costs of dry cleaning and repair

- Equipment like phones, computers, TVs, headphones, printers, disc drives. Separate the personal and business use

- Makeup you use for auditions and jobs or a percentage of a haircut you get specifically for a headshot session, an audition, a performance or industry event

- Costs of maintaining skills: for example, acting classes, singing lessons

- Expenses for your dressing room and gratuities paid to dressers and stage-door keepers

- Solely acting-related travel (consult the HMRC guidelines)

- Costs while touring or filming away from home

- A portion of your rent or mortgage (consult the HMRC guidelines)

- Bank charges and interest on a business account related to acting

Definitely on the 'NOT ALLOWABLE!' list:

- Any expense that is fully personally related, that is, you can't make a reasonable case for it to be included

- Expenses related to a PAYE job

- Reimbursements and per diems (the money you're given to cover living costs while away touring or filming). These count as income. Anything acting-related you spend your per diems on counts as an expense

- Entertaining; that is, paying for a meal/drinks for another person related to the industry
- Gifts for other people
- Drama school or uni fees

National Insurance

NI contributions go towards your state pension and other benefits. You can check your NI record online (if you don't have an HMRC online account yet, follow the advice on page 197).

- Class 1 NI: Comes out of PAYE jobs
- Class 2 NI: If your acting profits are over approx. £6,000, then Class 2 NI is charged as a lump sum of approx. £150 to be paid by the following 31 January
- Class 4 NI: Calculated as a percentage of your acting profits, over a certain threshold. For 2018/19 the percentage is 9 per cent on any profit you made above approx. £8,400

Student loans

You only make repayments on student loans if you're earning above a certain amount in a given tax year, and the amount you pay back depends on which type of loan you have. If you're not sure what plan you're on then go to studentloanrepayment.co.uk. This site has lots of clear advice, and you can set up an online account to check your balance, make extra payments and see how much interest you're paying.

HMRC will calculate how much you owe each year you fill out a self-assessment form. Any repayment made from your acting income will be taken after the tax year, at the same time as you pay your tax and NI. If you've worked a non-acting PAYE job as well, then (if you're earning over a certain amount) repayments may have been taken out of those pay cheques.

Tax and self-employment to-do

You have to take responsibility given the system is what it is.
                        Actor, five (tax) years in the profession

This section covers everything you need to get your tax and other payments accurate and on time. Go to the summary on page 203 for a sample timeline to see how this all fits together. And remember, if you're a member of Equity, you can get access to free advice and casework support on tax, national insurance and benefit issues.

Register as self-employed

Ideally, you should register as soon as you begin looking for your first paid acting job. The deadline for registering is 5th October the following tax year.

Go to the HMRC website, phone them (0300 200 3504) or use your accountant if you already have one. Among other details, you'll be asked for the type of business (acting) and your business address (normally your home). At the same time as registering you will be given an online account with a username and password, and your Unique Tax Reference (UTR). Hold on to these!

Consider hiring an accountant

An accountant will save you time and reassure you that everything's being done correctly. You will also hopefully save money overall, especially if you have relatively complex income and expenses. An accountant is also recommended by actors if you find yourself in a last minute deadline panic!

The disadvantage, of course, is the cost. If you haven't earned much from acting in a tax year and/or you're sure you can fill in the return correctly yourself, then like several actors I spoke to, you can choose to save yourself the fees.

Most charge by the hour, in which case any fee they suggest upfront will be an estimate. Prices range hugely, from less than a hundred pounds up into the thousands. If your tax situation is fairly simple, the advice is choose someone reputable but relatively cheap. If your income and expenses are high or complicated, paying more may reassure you you're getting the best saving overall.

To find an accountant, most actors suggest speaking to other performers in a similar position. If you're an Equity member, they can supply you with a list of specialists. You can also easily search online or use listing guides such as the *Actors and Performers Yearbook*. Any accountant should give you a free, no-obligation meeting in person or over the phone to discuss your situation and what they might charge. It's also a good idea to find out what they expect of you in terms of record-keeping.

Keep records

Throughout each tax year, keep hold of any tax, NI and student loan information and documents.

For your income:

- Payslips and agent statements from acting income
- Payslips from any PAYE (non-acting) jobs
- Bank statements for all your accounts
- P45s. These are sent to you when you leave a PAYE job, detailing your pay, plus any tax, NI and student loan you've paid. If you lose this, check your P60 . . .
- Your P60. This slip must be sent out to you by your current PAYE employer by the end of the tax year (contact them if you don't receive your P60 by the following 1st June). If you've lost it request a new one well in advance of the tax return deadline

Also keep hold of any documents detailing savings (statements from your bank/building society), investments, pensions and any income from renting a room or property.

To keep records of your acting-related expenses, store your:

- Receipts for acting-related purchases/expenditure
- Bank statements

As already mentioned, you'll also need to hold on to your:

- Online gov.uk username and password. You'll receive these after you register for self-employment. If you lose them, contact HMRC, and be aware that it can take a few weeks to get hold of replacements

- Your UTR (Unique Taxpayer Reference), a ten-digit number. Again, you'll also receive this by post after you've registered for self-employment. You can find it on certain other letters sent out by HMRC and by signing into your online account

- NI number. This will be on your payslips, your P45 and P60, and you can find it through your online account

One actor told me, 'I bundle all my receipts and payslips and everything else into a couple of envelopes and then when it's time, send it all off for the accountant to deal with.' Alternatively, another actor outlines a little-and-often approach to keeping records: 'I've got a deliberately little jar for keeping receipts in. As soon as it's full I type up the details on to my computer, then wait for the jar to fill again.' They then put everything together in a document box, with receipts in separate envelopes for each month of the tax year. In addition to this, they maintain a couple of spreadsheets or tables: one with acting income on it and another with expenses. Both are really simple:

Income spreadsheet mini-example

2018/19 Job		Date paid	Pay (before any agent fees)
	Romeo and Juliet	21/11/17	£350
	Doctors	28/02/18	£900
Total			£1,250

Expense spreadsheet mini-example

2018/19						
Date	Travel	Profess costs.	Office costs	Bank acc.	Other	Notes
Oct 2			70			Agent fee
Oct 4	8					Travel to TV job
Oct 5			7			% of mobile bill
Total =	...	...	...	...	...	...

Going through receipts and putting together spreadsheets is obviously quite dull but by spreading the workload over the year you can avoid a mad rush come the end of January. And if you're using an accountant, well-organized records may save you money; always ask how they prefer your accounts to be presented.

One final note here. Store your expenses records – including hard copy receipts – for at least five years after the filing deadline of 31 January after each tax year; for example, for the 2018/19 tax year, save receipts for at least five years from January 2020.

Save money

When the time comes for you to make a payment, you'll not only be covering tax owed but possibly also NI contributions and student loan repayments. One actor describes the safest way to make sure you're not caught out by a big bill: 'I have two accounts, and every acting job that has a weekly wage I put 20% of my money into a standing order going from my current account to my savings account. Then I leave it alone!' (Be aware that this 20 per cent here is only a useful guideline figure, and that going into higher tax thresholds will mean upping the percentage you're saving. Also see 'Make payments' on page 201.) If you're represented, you can make this system even more failsafe by asking your agent to split your payments into two different accounts.

A lot of actors I spoke to of course aren't as disciplined as that particular interviewee, and for some it's not necessarily the right approach. If you're having a quiet year acting-wise and paying tax through working PAYE jobs, for example, then there may be no need to save your acting earnings for tax.

Fill in the form

Once you hit the end of the tax year in April, you have until January 31st of the following calendar year to file your tax return (complete the online form) and make any payments you owe.

Many actors I spoke to told me they often end up doing everything in a bit of a panic right at the end of January. But as one organized performer highlights, 'you have all the information you'll need by 5th to do your tax return in April. You will know then nine months ahead how much you will have to pay in the following January, and you don't have to rush.' If you've hired an accountant, they'll fill in the self-assessment form for you. Get your receipts and records to them with at least a few weeks' notice (you may be able to save fees – and certainly some stress – by getting your records to your accountant as early as possible).

If you're filling in the form yourself, add up your expenses using the categories listed. 'Turnover' (in the self-employment section) is your total pay for all the acting work over the tax year, before any agent fees, pension contributions or other deductions. In the self-employed section, your business description will be 'Actor'. The date your books or accounts is made up to is 5th April of the tax year you're filing the return for. If you've had a second job, use the information on your P60 or P45 to complete the employment section of the form. To fill in the section on student loan repayments from employment jobs consult your P45 and/or P60. If you've recorded a loss from acting work, you can fill in the boxes to reduce a current, or previous or future year's tax bill (this can get complicated, and it may be worth consulting an accountant if you're unsure).

Many of the questions on the form won't be relevant; if you're unsure, click the question marks next to each box. If you're still unsure, there are guidelines on the HMRC website, and if you're an Equity member, you can contact their tax experts for help.

Make payments

The first deadline for paying money owed for a tax year is 31st January of the following calendar year. Once you've filled in the form HMRC will tell you how much you owe and give you payment options. Missing HMRC deadlines means paying fines.

You may also have to make payments on account: two payments in advance for your next tax bill, one by Jan 31st and one by July 31st. Each of these payments is half of your total acting-related tax bill, a sort of prediction of what you will pay for your next tax year. The idea is that you are spreading out payments for your future tax bill, rather than having to pay it in one big hit.

You don't have to make payments on account if your self-employed tax payment is going to be lower than £1,000; nor do you if 80 per cent of your entire tax bill is being paid through PAYE. However, if you've earned a fair chunk of your salary through acting during your first tax year in the profession, or if your earnings dramatically increase suddenly at any point in your career, you will more than likely have to pay a decent-sized amount on account. To avoid being caught out make sure you're saving enough throughout each year (see page 200).

If you are worried you won't be able to make your payments on account then you (using the SA303 form online) or your accountant can contact HMRC to have them reduced or even cancelled. The same goes if you think your earnings are likely to be dramatically less the following tax year. This can be complicated and there are fines if you get things wrong, so if you have an accountant follow their advice on this; if you don't and you're really unsure consider hiring one.

Consider protecting yourself against investigation

HMRC will occasionally pick out an actor's accounts to investigate: either at random or because they spot something odd. An investigation can go on for months, and all in all it can be, as one actor I spoke to describes, 'a complete arse'.

If HMRC do investigate, they may not find anything wrong, and as one actor says, even if you've been doing your accounts yourself, you won't get into trouble 'if you have reasoning behind your expenses ... if you were investigated, then at least you can explain yourself'. To avoid having to spend hundreds of pounds on accountant fees, you can purchase insurance in case of investigation. Many accountants offer their own version of this, as does Equity, which is cheaper than most.

Tax and self-employment timeline

The table below gives an overview of tax and self-employment tasks to complete and deadlines to hit, summing up key points from this chapter. The dates and info are based on an actor leaving a drama course during the 2018/19 tax year.

Date	PAYE tasks	Self-employment tasks
6th Apr '18: 2018/19 tax year begins		Begin keeping 18/19 tax records incl. startup cost receipts Earliest point to register as self-employed Safely store usernames, passwords and UTR
Jul '18: Finish drama course		
Sep '18: First paid acting job		
Nov '18: Begins temp job		
Jan '19: Finishes temp job	Keep P45	
Feb '19: Second paid acting job		
5th Apr '19: 2018/19 tax year ends	Keep P60	
6th Apr '19: 2019/20 tax year begins		Earliest point to file first return, make payment (and possible payments on account) Begin keeping records for 19/20
5th Oct '19:		Deadline to register as self-employed
Early Jan '20:		If using an accountant, last chance to send records
31st Jan '20:		Deadline to file return and make first payment, and first payment on account if applicable Earliest point to make second payment on account
5th Apr '20: 19/20 tax year ends	Keep P60	
6th Apr '20: 20/21 tax year begins		Earliest point to file return and make payments for 2020/21
31st Jul '20		Deadline for making second payment on account (if applicable)

Disclaimer:

The points raised in this chapter are correct at the time of publication but may be subject to change. No responsibility for loss by any person acting or refraining from action as a result of this chapter can be accepted; nor can any legal liability be assumed for any errors or admissions this article may contain.

For free resources to help you make the most of the expert advice in this chapter, visit www.actorscareerbible.com/freestuff